Becoming
REAL

And Thriving in Ministry

Becoming
REAL

And Thriving in Ministry

SANDRA T. MONTES

CHURCH
PUBLISHING
INCORPORATED

Church Publishing
19 East 34th Street
New York, NY 10016
www.churchpublishing.org

Cover design by Mark Whitaker, MTWdesign
Typeset by Rose Design

Library of Congress Cataloging-in-Publication Data

Names: Montes, Sandra, author.
Title: Becoming REAL and thriving in ministry / Sandra Montes.
Identifiers: LCCN 2020000306 (print) | LCCN 2020000307 (ebook) | ISBN 9781640652484 (paperback) | ISBN 9781640652491 (epub)
Subjects: LCSH: Pastoral theology. | Church growth. | Church work with Hispanic Americans.
Classification: LCC BV4011.3 .M655 2020 (print) | LCC BV4011.3 (ebook) | DDC 253--dc23
LC record available at https://lccn.loc.gov/2020000306
LC ebook record available at https://lccn.loc.gov/2020000307

For papi and mami
who taught me how to be real con su ejemplo.

Contents

Why REAL

have been in the Church from the moment I was in my parents' thoughts and prayers. My parents met in Bible school, where both had a call to go into ministry. My mom says she always prayed to be a pastor's wife and my dad says he felt the call into ordained ministry when he was young. We were in the Christian Missionary Alliance Church until the late '80s when we, dramatically, found the Episcopal Church (more on that story later).

From the moment I could form a thought, I saw so many ways people could improve their churches. Some, like my parents, call this discernment, while others call this being *criticona*, a critic. I'm sure it's a combination of both. I noticed when things were out of place. I noticed when things were dirty. I noticed when people were using poor photocopies. I noticed when the hymn of the day did not match the hymn posted on the wall or printed in the bulletin. I noticed bigger things, too, as I was growing. I noticed that I was not allowed to sing songs that I had written because leading music was a man's job. I noticed that women could be Sunday school teachers in my evangelical church, but could not be pastors. I noticed that everyone at the altar was a white male. I noticed that while some churches dwindled in numbers, the neighborhoods in which these churches were located were vibrant and populous.

I have been forming opinions about everything church related for years. I have been listening, observing, researching, and searching for what works since I could read the Bible. I have seen successful churches and churches that needed help. I have had conversations about the church at least weekly since I could speak. Little by little, I started noticing some things my dad did in San Mateo, an Episcopal parish in Houston, Texas. Although I saw my dad succeed in Guatemala, McAllen, Harlingen, and Houston, because he taught by example, most of the concepts that I have analyzed for this book came from his work at Iglesia Episcopal San Mateo, the first all-Latino Episcopal parish in the United States. Because we were in San Mateo for thirty years, I saw my dad grow from a layperson to a deacon, a priest, and finally, a rector. At the same time, I saw San Mateo growing in faith, commitment, numbers, giving, and outreach.

I later realized all successful pastors (and really any successful person I know) do four things in various ways and to various degrees. It sounds simple, and the concepts, or values, are very simple. But the application, commitment, hard work, and patience they take are not for those who want a quick fix or easy results.

I have called these observations and realizations by many different names throughout the years. Having taught for over twenty years, I love a good mnemonic, and REAL became the culmination of what I have observed and learned about the Church: respectful relationships, excellence, authenticity, and love. Like a healthy lifestyle—which I am still learning to embrace—REAL takes time and a bit of trial and error before you see the results. Once you start seeing results, though, and find the motivation to continue the course, it is incredibly rewarding.

I consider relationships the most important part of church work because that is what I saw in my church. I have been outspoken about authenticity wherever I am invited to speak, write, or sing and across social media. I have talked about God's unconditional love from the moment I started needing it . . . or, rather, from the moment I started messing up so much that I truly needed to know God would love me no matter what and forgives all. I have tried to do everything I do for God with excellence. Because I have great role models in my parents, who pray for me and encourage me, I have tried to speak truth in love. This isn't always easy.

Because I was part of the only all–*gente Latina* self-sustaining church in the United States for about thirty years, I am frequently asked what is the key to church growth and to church vitality. I am often invited to speak on evangelism, discipleship, and stewardship, three significant areas for the church today.*

REAL began to manifest its realness. Sonny Browne invited me to sing, along with my friend Jamey Graves, and speak at the East Carolina diocesan convention in February 2017. As I was preparing, I decided to expand on REAL. After my talk, Sonny encouraged me to write this book.

As I continued to share these important values with others, I realized that whenever I visited a church, I noticed things that could be improved easily but could have a lasting and meaningful outcome. I did not have a church home at the time and I decided to visit a different church each week in 2018—as much as I could. My learnings and experiences found their way into blog posts, articles, and talks as I traveled around the Episcopal Church.

I have used REAL when working with churches, schools, and other organizations. I use REAL when talking about diversity, racial competence, and many other topics. I encourage you to use REAL as a framework when starting any ministry and when working to include those who may not currently enter through your church doors.

I hope that you will see Jesus all over REAL, even if he is not in the acronym. REAL would not be possible if Jesus was not at the center of it all. As Christians, everything we do is because of our love for Jesus and our obedience to love God above all, love our neighbor, and love ourselves. Jesus is the reason I can say that

---

* Because many words in Spanish are gendered, I try to use words and phrases that do not need a gender. For example, instead of using *Latinx* all the time, because it may be confusing or unwelcoming to some *gente latina*, I prefer using *gente latina* or *la gente latina*. *Gente Latina* is also used by many of us and includes people from Spain or the Caribbean.

REAL can be life changing. When we are open to the Spirit of God, we can achieve many things that seem impossible. I can see God's hands all over my journey and the inspiration to put what I have learned into four letters.

I am constantly challenging the Church to be REAL. I am constantly calling people to look inside and outside of themselves and of their organizations or churches and see if they are being authentic and diverse. One of my favorite activities is to ask people to take out their phones. I ask them to check out their last ten or twenty pictures. Those not only tell a story but will reflect if we are truly living into the two commandments Jesus called most important. My second favorite activity is to ask people to check out their social media pages and see what they are posting. That also gives us a glimpse as to what is important to us. Some people will share their meals, weight loss, and a million selfies but feel very uncomfortable sharing something about their church. Now, before we become self-righteous or self-loathing, what could we, as church leaders, do that is exciting or amazing or life changing enough that people are moved to share? It is easy to say that people don't want to share their faith on social media, but we share whatever we find we can't live without. I believe we have something better than apple pie, better than the best shoes, the best movie, the best song. We have Jesus. How can I encourage others to feel that excited about their relationship with Jesus?

We often hear that the church is dying, which may not be a problem since we are children of the resurrection. It seems we are so afraid of what would happen if we laid down our lives and trusted God. How about those of us inside the walls of the church encourage or infect others with our enthusiasm? We may be dying, we may be passing through a Good (or bad) Friday. But Sunday is coming.

I pray that, as you read about REAL, you will be encouraged. I pray that you will see how your respectful relationships, excellence, authenticity, and love can change someone's life and can transform your congregation. I pray that you can find new ways of using REAL as a tool for determining where ministries or personal goals can use a review and fresh consideration.

I pray that you will see that you are not alone in this beautiful pilgrimage of ministry. I pray that you will note that the examples can work for anyone anywhere. I pray that you have many epiphanies and surprises and much joy as you read what others are doing around the church.

One pro tip: although it may seem that you can skip one of the four values, please do an inventory. These values don't have to be done in order, but they do build on each other. When one value is skipped, the others don't seem to fall into place.

If you have never participated in anything like this, please start with respectful relationships. If your church is going through a difficult time, start with devoting time to building respectful relationships within your own parish before going out into the world in peace. That old adage about putting on your own mask first before helping others in case of an emergency during a flight works for this as well. You can't give what you don't have. Jesus says: love God, love yourself, love others.

Sandra, that's not what that verse says. You're right. Again, the teacher comes out and I take context clues. How are you supposed to love others "like you love yourself" if you don't love yourself first? I grew up in the evangelical church where I was taught JOY: Jesus, others, you. I always wondered about that. I felt like we were missing something. We were encouraged to put others before ourselves every time. I understand that we must put others first in some instances, but that has nothing to do with love. I can love me and still put your needs first. I can also love me and put my needs before anyone else's. That is not love. That is selfishness. We are, however, commanded to love ourselves.

As we work toward respectful relationships, let's find opportunities to spend time with each other having deep, intimate,
transparent conversations about what is going on in our churches
and why there is conflict. You may want to do what the Bible
suggests: go to the person or persons and try to resolve the issue.
If that doesn't work, bring a few others (members of the vestry,
maybe?) to talk to the person. A parish-wide conversation may
also be very helpful: I am certain that individuals feel the stress
and awkwardness of issues not being mentioned. Often, when
we confront a problem immediately, we can stop the spread of
gossip or bad feelings. Not always, and not all the gossip, but it is
always better to confront a situation and begin the conversations
or actions that are necessary to heal.

After having those conversations that will bring a deeper
connection and relationship, parishes are better prepared for the
mission to reach the rest of the world. Some have tried this and
still failed to get to a healthy place. I call them "in therapy." They
are people who may not be at their healthiest, but they are taking
the medicine—or measures—to get to a healthier place. They
are doing the work of conversation, time, prayer, Bible study,
commitment to the community. They are also actively working
not to spread hate or bitterness.

This work is tough. This is not something that can happen in
a day. It takes, as everything in ministry, tenacity, love, and commitment. We cannot give up. This work of evangelizing, of making disciples, and of forming new Christians takes great amounts
of time and energy. If we give up when things get a little tough, we
will not reach the goal. We must ask God to arm us with tenacity. Nothing will happen if we don't have love. If we are not doing
everything in love, we are missing out on the beauty of giving.
When we have love, we have it all. We can do anything, we can
bear anything, we can stick with it. And lastly, commitment. I am
divorced. I know what it is like to have made promises that could

not be kept. Now, I can see that I have remained committed to that relationship because we have a son and I remain committed to being a parent with my ex-husband to the child we share.

REAL is not going to be able to change anything unless you have people who are committed to seeing it through. The goal is to have the leadership committed to being REAL. What does this mean? It means that the lay and ordained leadership of a church must trust that respectful relationships, excellence, authenticity, and love will help transform their church and community. We must first trust the values in REAL and then pray that God prepares the soil for our sowing.

REAL is not a cure-all, although I must admit it has helped me with all of my relationships, commitments, jobs, and ministries. When I notice that something is not going quite right, I ask myself which of the four values in REAL is lagging. I live in a multicultural, multilingual, and diverse world. I know that if I am not following the rubric of REAL, I may not be able to thrive in my community or the other communities of which I am a part.

Why would you want to put yourself out there, with the possibility of being mocked or turned away? Why would you want to reach out to a different demographic than what is already in your church? Why would you risk losing people who are already in your church just because there are people who are different in your surrounding community? Why open the doors to people who may not have the same educational background or financial stability as those in your pews? Why do all the work without any guarantee of success?

If your answer to any of those questions did not include the words "called," "call," or "calling," please rethink your motivations. There are too many people longing to hear the word of God, to hear that they are loved unconditionally, and to believe that someone chooses them and calls them friends. Those of us who are part of the marginalized, the outcast, the other, long for people who will continue to help us and show us Jesus's love: his true, unpopular, extremely free love.

I pray that REAL answers many of your questions. I am hopeful that when you finish reading this book you will find a reason to apply REAL to your community or congregation. You are not alone. There are many people who share your hopes, dreams, or goals. I would love to help you reach your goals of becoming a welcoming, open, inclusive community.

Capítulo 1: El porqué de REAL

He estado en la Iglesia desde el momento en que estuve en los pensamientos y oraciones de mis padres. Mis padres se conocieron en un instituto bíblico en el Perú, donde ambos tenían un llamado para entrar al ministerio. Mi mami dice que siempre oró para ser la esposa de un pastor y mi papi dice que sintió el llamado al ministerio ordenado cuando era joven. Estuvimos en la Iglesia Alianza Cristiana y Misionera hasta finales de los 80 cuando, dramáticamente, encontramos la Iglesia Episcopal (esa historia la explico más adelante).

Desde el momento en que pude formarme un pensamiento, vi muchas maneras en que las personas podían mejorar sus iglesias. Algunas personas, como mis padres, llaman esto discernimiento, mientras que otras lo llaman ser criticona. Estoy segura de que es una combinación. Me daba cuenta cuando las cosas estaban fuera de lugar. Me daba cuenta cuando las cosas estaban desarregladas y sucias. También notaba cosas mayores a medida que crecía. Notaba que no se me permitía cantar cantos que había escrito porque estar al frente de una iglesia era un ministerio para hombres. Notaba que las mujeres podían ser maestras de escuela dominical en mi iglesia evangélica, pero no podían ser pastoras. Notaba que todos los que servían en el altar eran hombres blancos. Notaba que mientras algunas iglesias disminuían en número, los vecindarios en los que se ubicaban estas iglesias eran vibrantes y poblados.

He estado formándome opiniones sobre todo lo relacionado con la Iglesia durante años. He estado escuchando, observando, investigando y buscando lo que funciona desde que podía leer la Biblia. He visto iglesias exitosas e iglesias que necesitaban ayuda. He tenido conversaciones sobre la Iglesia al menos semanalmente desde que aprendí a hablar. Poco a poco, comencé a notar algunas cosas que hacía mi papi. Aunque vi a mi papi triunfar en Guatemala, McAllen, Harlingen y Houston, porque siempre ha enseñado con su ejemplo, la mayoría de los conceptos que he analizado para este libro provienen de su trabajo en la Iglesia Episcopal San Mateo, la primera parroquia episcopal totalmente latina en los Estados Unidos. Debido a que estuvimos en San Mateo durante treinta años, vi a mi papi crecer de laico a diácono, sacerdote y, finalmente, rector. Al mismo tiempo, vi a San Mateo crecer en fe, compromiso, números, ofrendas y alcance. Después, me di cuenta de que todos los pastores exitosos (y realmente cualquier persona exitosa que conozco) hacen estas cuatro cosas de varias maneras. Suena simple, y los conceptos, o valores, son muy simples. Pero la aplicación, el compromiso, el trabajo y la paciencia que toman no son para las personas que desean una solución rápida o resultados fáciles.

He llamado a estas observaciones y comprensiones por muchos nombres diferentes a lo largo de los años. El acrónimo REAL se convirtió en la culminación de lo que he observado y aprendido sobre un ministerio exitoso: relaciones respetuosas, excelencia, amor y ser legítimo. Al igual que un estilo de vida saludable, que todavía estoy aprendiendo a adoptar, REAL requiere tiempo y un poco de prueba antes de ver los resultados.

Considero que las relaciones son la parte más importante del trabajo de la iglesia porque eso es lo que vi en mi iglesia. He sido franca sobre la autenticidad dondequiera que me invitan a hablar, escribir o cantar y en las redes sociales. He hablado sobre el amor incondicional de Dios desde el momento en que comencé a necesitarlo . . . , o más bien, desde el momento en que comencé a equivocarme tanto que realmente necesité saber que Dios me amaba y perdonaba sin importar lo que hiciera o hubiese hecho. He tratado de hacer todo lo que hago para Dios con excelencia. Debido a que tengo excelentes modelos a seguir en mis padres que oran por mí y me animan, he tratado de decir la verdad en amor. Eso no siempre ha sido fácil.

Debido a que formé parte de la única iglesia latina autosustentable (gente de América Latina) en los Estados Unidos durante aproximadamente treinta años, a menudo me preguntan la clave para el crecimiento y la vitalidad de la iglesia. A menudo me piden que hable sobre evangelismo, discipulado y mayordomía, tres áreas importantes para la Iglesia.

Sonny Browne me invitó a cantar, junto con mi amigo Jamey Graves, y hablar en la convención diocesana de Carolina del Este en febrero de 2017. Mientras me preparaba, decidí desarrollar un poco más el concepto de REAL. Y cuando Sonny me escuchó me dijo una y otra vez que debería escribir un libro sobre REAL.

Mientras compartía estos importantes valores con otras personas, me di cuenta de que cada vez que visitaba una iglesia, notaba cosas que podrían mejorarse fácilmente y que podrían tener un resultado duradero y significativo. No tenía una iglesia en ese entonces y decidí visitar, siempre que pude, una iglesia diferente cada semana durante el 2018. Esos aprendizajes y experiencias se materializaron en mi blog, como artículos y charlas mientras viajaba por la Iglesia Episcopal.

He usado REAL cuando trabajo con iglesias, escuelas y otras organizaciones. Uso REAL cuando hablo de diversidad, competencia racial y muchos otros temas. Animo a las personas a usar REAL como marco de referencia al comenzar cualquier ministerio y al tratar de incluir a aquellas personas que actualmente no entran por las puertas de su iglesia.

Espero que puedas ver a Jesús presente en todo este libro. REAL no sería posible si Jesús no estuviera en el centro de todo. Como personas cristianas, todo lo que hacemos es por nuestro amor a Jesús y nuestra obediencia en amar a Dios sobre todas las cosas, amar a nuestro prójimo y amarnos a nosotros mismos. Jesús es la razón por la que puedo afirmar que REAL cambia vidas. Cuando estamos abiertos al Espíritu de Dios, podemos lograr muchas cosas que parecen imposibles. Puedo ver las manos de Dios en todo mi trayecto y en la inspiración para poner lo que he aprendido en cuatro letras.

Constantemente desafío a la Iglesia a ser REAL. Constantemente llamo a las personas a mirar dentro y fuera de sí mismas y de sus organizaciones o iglesias y ver si son auténticas y diversas.

A menudo escuchamos que la iglesia—especialmente la Iglesia Episcopal en los Estados Unidos, particularmente la parte de habla inglesa—se está muriendo, y tal vez no es un problema ya que somos hijos e hijas de la resurrección. Parece que tenemos tanto miedo de lo que sucedería si confiamos en Dios aun con nuestra muerte.

Oro para que, mientras leas este libro, te animes. Oro para que veas cómo tus relaciones respetuosas, la excelencia, el amor y el ser legítimos pueden cambiar la vida de alguien y transformar tu congregación. Mi anhelo es que puedas encontrar nuevas formas de usar REAL como una herramienta en tu ministerio. Espero que tengas muchas epifanías, sorpresas y alegrías mientras lees lo que otras personas están haciendo en la Iglesia.

Un consejo profesional: aunque parezca que se puede omitir uno de los cuatro valores, haz un inventario. Estos valores no tienen que hacerse en orden, sino que se entrelazan. Cuando se omite un valor, los otros no parecen encajar. Si nunca has participado en algo similar, comienza con relaciones respetuosas.

Este trabajo es difícil. Se necesita, como todo en el ministerio, tenacidad, amor y compromiso. No podemos rendirnos. Esta obra de evangelización, de hacer discípulos y de formar nuevos cristianos requiere una gran cantidad de tiempo y energía. Si nos rendimos cuando las cosas se ponen un poco difíciles, no alcanzaremos la meta. Debemos pedirle a Dios que nos equipe con tenacidad. No pasará nada si no tenemos amor. Cuando tenemos amor, lo tenemos todo.

REAL no podrá cambiar nada a menos que tengas personas comprometidas a hacerlo. El objetivo es tener el liderazgo comprometido a ser REAL. ¿Qué significa esto? Significa que el liderazgo laico y ordenado de una iglesia debe confiar en que las relaciones respetuosas, la excelencia, el amor y el ser legítimos ayudarán a transformar tu iglesia y comunidad. Primero debemos confiar en los valores de REAL y luego orar para que Dios prepare todo para nuestra siembra.

REAL no es un remedio, aunque debo admitir que me ha ayudado con todas mis relaciones, compromisos, trabajos y ministerios. Cuando noto que algo no va bien, me pregunto cuál de los cuatro valores de REAL está siendo ignorado.

Somos llamados a llevar las buenas nuevas a todo el mundo. Hay demasiadas personas que anhelan escuchar la palabra de Dios, escuchar que son amadas incondicionalmente y creer que alguien los elige y los llama por su nombre. Las personas que somos parte de los grupos marginados anhelamos personas que continúen ayudándonos y mostrándonos el amor de Jesús: su amor verdadero, impopular y extremadamente libre.

Oro para que REAL responda muchas de tus preguntas. Tengo la esperanza de que cuando termines de leer este libro encuentres una razón para utilizar REAL en tu comunidad o congregación. No estás solo; no estás sola. Hay muchas personas que comparten tus esperanzas, sueños u objetivos. Me encantaría ayudarte a alcanzar tus objetivos de que tu iglesia, congregación o comunidad de fe sea una comunidad hospitalaria, abierta e inclusiva.

CHAPTER 2

Respectful Relationships

I can do all things.
I can break away any shackle and make mountains disappear.
I can do all things through Christ who strengthens me.

"I Can Do All Things" / "Todo lo puedo hacer"
—text and tune by Sandra T. Montes

Throughout my life, I have seen the importance of relationships. When I was four, my family moved from our home country of Perú to Guatemala, where my dad was going to attend seminary. We did not have any family or friends in Guatemala and our relationships with each other grew stronger because we had to rely only on each other for everything. Today, I still have a very strong bond with my parents and brother that goes back to that time of significant relationship building. Relationships will get us where we need or want to go but developing them is not a fast process. Building relationships takes time, energy, effort, and intentionality. Building respectful relationships is hard work and very rewarding.

People often say that they would like more youth, families, people of color, multicultural, multilingual folks in their organizations or churches. When I ask why, the answer often says a lot about the beliefs and commitment behind the comment. If you have said, "I would like to have more youth in our church," or something like it, allow yourself to take some time to rest and meditate on the "why." Has God put that group in your heart for a reason? Have you looked around your neighborhood and felt that group isn't being served? If your answer has nothing to do with growing in Spirit and sharing Jesus's love with others, you may want to reassess why you want to include more of that group, that language, or that culture in your church. Once we have determined that yes, our quest for opening our doors and hearts is spirit led, we can move forward.

As church leaders, our job, after evangelizing, is to be present and visible in our communities. I encourage leaders to look at a one-mile radius around their church, organization, or home. Take a prayer walk alone or with a group around that radius. In other words, as you walk, meditate on a mantra, Bible verse, or prayers (the Book of Common Prayer has great ones). You can also stop at stop signs or corners and pray aloud or sing a song. As you walk and pray, jot down everyone and everything you see. What kind of services are provided for the neighborhood and its residents? Are there young families? Are there many youth and children? Are there schools, daycares, other education-focused entities? Are there places where people can congregate, like a park or a public garden? Can people safely walk within this radius? Then, look at your church or organization as you and your group consider follow-up questions and meditation (see the activities at the end of the chapter for more instructions and questions).

Once you finish your prayer walk, use your data to help you proceed with the next step. If your next step includes that group you are longing for—youth, young families, people who speak another language, refugees, people who have other abilities— then start thinking about establishing respectful relationships with them. If your walk and God are directing you to another group, thank God for the insight and prepare a plan for that group, always starting with respectful relationships.

Relationships, even when they seem easy and fast in this fast-paced society, take time to solidify. They also take commitment, compromise, forgiveness, and effort. I have seen people try to make friendships or relationships with just a few minutes together, often starting these through the internet, apps, or at a conference. That is almost impossible. For us to get to know each other, we must invest time in the relationship. We must be interested in getting to know another person. We have to make a choice and an effort when seeking to start relationships with others. This is not easy, but does pay off in the end.

The first step you can take when you want to begin a relationship with a group of individuals (youth, young family, different ethnic group, etc.) is to go where they are (see the chapter activities about creating and sharing a neighborhood resource map).

If you are looking to build relationships with youth, start where they spend the greatest amount of time: school. Is there a junior high or high school nearby? Are there junior high or high school teachers in your congregation? Do you have at least a couple of youth you could start a relationship with? If the answer is yes to any of these, great! You can start building those relationships by showing up, by being present, by starting the conversation with people who are either part of that community or who can take you to them. If the answer is no to most of these, then you may want to reevaluate your target group. Are youth truly the group you are being called to serve (recall your prayer walk)? Maybe your community is filled with older adults and that group of individuals is a place to begin building relationships.

Once you have decided where those you feel called to reach and serve spend time, start visiting those places. Relationships take time, and when you are seeking to build relationships with individuals who are not already in your organization or church, it may be more difficult to start them organically. You must show up for people for them to start trusting you. You must be genuinely interested in them, what they need and like. How can you find out their wants or needs? Ask them. Do not assume you know what the needs are.

If you already have members from the neighborhood in your congregation, start nurturing those relationships before branching out. If you hope to reach youth, attend their sports games, go to their graduations, make time to speak with their parents and share with them what your vision is. If you have young families and have decided that is the group God is calling you to minister to, visit them or invite them to the park where you can have an unstructured, friendly conversation.

As you are getting to know individuals and developing respectful relationships, listen actively. Do not try to sell them on your church or your beliefs. Allow them to ask questions and provide as much information, resources, direction as needed, when asked.

Once you start with initial conversations to get to know each other, the opportunity will come to ask about wants and needs. There is nothing more powerful than being asked what we want or long for and knowing that the other person is listening and happy to help us get there.

It is important to remember that establishing respectful relationships as part of an evangelism effort is not so that the people you're spending time with will come to church and become parishioners, but rather it is to show them Jesus and God's love. Many people can recognize when someone is being fake, so be mindful of that when you are offering your respectful relationship or friendship. Understand why you are taking the time to establish a respectful relationship and understand why it's important to your church or organization. Before and as your congregation is working to establish respectful relationships, offer training on how to evangelize and how to start a respectful relationship.

While your conversation shouldn't sound practiced, memorized, or robotized, it is useful for those who are participating in these opportunities for building respectful relationships to be prepared with basic information on your organization or church, denomination, beliefs, and how to establish great conversations.

People in respectful relationships know that we are not all going to think the same or agree all the time. We all come with different experiences, cultures, and beliefs. That is why when we are starting these respectful relationships, listening is essential. We must create spaces for communication and ongoing conversations. We must look for opportunities to build relationships in our communities. When we are prepared, we will know where we can go, where we can have opportunities to speak, conversation starters, and overall best conversation practices.

I have seen groups try to start a new service or have a neighborhood event or church-wide conference; they will have worked diligently to provide the perfect music, the perfect food, the perfect place, and have done it all with a lot of love. But because they have not started by building respectful relationships and truly don't know what people want or need, the event completely flops. Those who organize these events feel discouraged and many want to give up. When we begin by building respectful relationships and then take the opportunity to ask those with whom we are in relationship what they may need or want—in an event or church service or something entirely different—we may find that they are looking for something unlike what we had presumed. That is why respectful relationships come first.

My dad, a retired Episcopal priest who was the first rector of an all-Latino, self-supporting parish in the United States, came into the Church through a respectful relationship. He ran away from home when he was a child because of physical abuse. He was homeless and survived by breaking the law against stealing food. When he was a teenager, he began working for a Christian family who took him in and loved him. They always invited him to go to church with them and he always said no. However, through their relationship, as the family nurtured him and met his needs of food, shelter, and a job, he eventually agreed to attend a service. When he finally went to church with the family, his life changed. They didn't force him into attending, they didn't threaten him, they invited him, after having built a respectful relationship with him.

After a while, my dad felt a call to ministry and went to Bible college, where he met my mom. They planted a few churches in Perú and then my dad went to seminary in Guatemala. After graduation, he was invited to several countries and decided to move to the United States. While he was a Christian Missionary Alliance pastor living in the Rio Grande Valley of Texas, he attended an ecumenical Evangelism Explosion conference in New York City. There, he met Hugo Pina, an Episcopal bishop. Years later, my dad was delivering pizzas (not earning enough money as a pastor) when he was robbed, beaten, and left for dead. At the hospital, he called the senior pastor at the church where he was working, who told my dad to call him when he was back home. My dad was saddened and felt alone. He remembered meeting this bishop, who lived in Houston, years earlier at the conference in New York. Looking through his wallet, my dad found his business card. He called Bishop Pina, who answered but told my dad he couldn't come see him—my dad's heart sank—because he had a *quinceañera*, but he would come as soon as the event was over.

My dad always remembers seeing Bishop Pina running into his room still wearing his beautiful episcopal attire. They had started their relationship years before, not knowing that God would bring them back together in this tragic situation. My dad began helping Bishop Pina at St. Matthew's/San Mateo as his sexton, then started helping with music and Bible study. One day, Bishop Pina said to my dad, "Alejandro, God has called you to deliver the good news, not to deliver pizza," and that is how my dad's journey into the Episcopal Church began. All because of a respectful relationship begun at a conference and solidified because Bishop Pina felt it was important to be present where my dad was.

People are hurting all over the world. People need us to go where they are and take Jesus with us. People need relationships rooted in respect, patience, love, and commitment. People need those relationships that can transform them and us. I can't imagine what would have happened if Bishop Pina hadn't gone to see my dad. I can't imagine what would have happened if my dad had remained in a conservative and traditional evangelical denomination instead of coming into one that is more open and progressive. It was the respectful relationship that Obispo Pina and my dad built that helped them both imagine a future where my dad, an evangelical pastor, could lead an Episcopal community built by Roman Catholic immigrants.

Churches must decide if they will simply go through the motions of having a nice Sunday morning liturgy, or if they will be Jesus, building relationships without concern for how long individuals may attend the church. Some people are looking for a special service, like a baptism, *quinceañera*, or wedding, and are not looking for a church home—or may not know they are. (*Quinceañera* means fifteen-year-old. Traditionally, it is a special birthday party that mostly girls celebrate in Latina culture. Not all Spanish-speaking countries celebrate it and not all Latinas celebrate it.) As part of our call to evangelism and community engagement, we can share our church as a resource for people to celebrate and learn a bit more about Jesus and our church. Remember the parable of the sower. We must always sow God's seed. God does the rest. How can we be Jesus, sowing the seed of a relationship?

Time is one of the most important gifts we can give someone when we are building respectful relationships. Time shows interest. When we devote time to others, we are saying that they matter and that we are committed to the relationship. Time is a precious commodity but by choosing our priorities, anyone can give it. By respecting the priorities, cultures, and responsibilities of those with whom we are building relationships, we can respect the time they are willing to give to us.

During the relationship building, we will notice that trust builds and grows. This trust does not happen overnight. This is especially true for those who have never been to church regularly or those who have been hurt by the Church. You may want to hint at your church connection from the first meeting. For example, when meeting someone near the church building, let them know that you attend "that church around the corner" and explain the denomination and congregation, if that seems appropriate. This does not need to be a catechesis lesson or a theological discussion but rather an introduction to your church and the importance it has for you.

Many pastors are concerned that their church is dying. Many pastors are concerned that the congregations they serve are older people who do not want to change. As I work with priests and pastors with these concerns, I suggest a prayer walk to see what is around their church. They sometimes tell me, "We know there are a lot of Hispanics but we don't know how to reach them." Part of establishing relationships with people is just going outside our walls. We will never know how to reach people if we don't take the first step of getting up, getting out, and getting involved with as many people as possible who often appear different from the people in our pews.

If it seems to you that your church is dying, but outside your doors the neighborhood is thriving, what does that say about your church? Has your congregation become a silo? Has it become a secret club where entrance depends on knowing someone already on the inside? Has your church become a "best-kept secret"? All of these point to the possibility that your church is not living up to the mandate to share the good news with all the world. Sometimes it is very comfortable to stay with our friends, family, and fellow parishioners that we've known for*ever*. We don't want to venture out, we like doing things like we have always done them. But, that is the best way to die.

I must admit that I am not opposed to the death of a church, congregation, or organization, especially when things are not going right or when there is illness and obvious decay. We are, after all, children of the resurrection. I've heard, "For there to be a Sunday, there must be a Friday," or "It's Friday but Sunday is coming," or "Death won't keep us down." All of these are true. It is all right to let something "die" because we know God will resurrect it and it will be triumphant. This does not mean that everything has to die in order for it to be saved; Jesus is a miracle worker and calls us to believe and share that belief. Jesus is also a relationship builder. There are many stories about his friends, about Jesus spending time with others, and about Jesus connecting everyone with his parent: God.

When you do look outside your doors, whether it's going on a prayer walk or simply looking around the neighborhood, seeing life and faces you've never noticed before, stop and thank God. Thank God for the opportunity to see your neighborhood and community as you never have before. It is always important to see things with new eyes. Maybe your habit is leaving immediately after church to meet friends or family for a meal or event. Maybe there is a local restaurant where the opportunity will arise to talk to people there about your church and about your faith. I know that may be scary, but it is usually scary only the first few times.

In the Episcopal Diocese of Arizona, then-Bishop Kirk Smith asked all of his pastors to be chaplains in the community. It didn't matter if they were chaplains of the local sports team or of the police department: he asked them to be among the people. They were also asked to be outside of the office and in the community. What a brilliant intentional invitation to be Church. Church is not only inside our walls; church often happens outside of them. Many priests and parish leaders are too busy to add a community chaplaincy on top of work schedules, so this mandate becoming part of their workweek is such a great call to evangelize and get to know people who need Jesus and God's love.

Kenneth Katona was vicar of St. Peter's Episcopal Church in Casa Grande in the diocese of Arizona when we met. Katona (as I call him) says that he loved the invitation to go outside of his church to volunteer as a chaplain because "people don't come into our churches because we paint the doors red . . . if we are going to engage with people for Jesus, we need to go to them." After conversations around the community, he met a firefighter who told him the fire department didn't have a chaplain. He went to each of the five fire stations in Casa Grande and began to develop a relationship with them. He did ride-alongs with each crew, riding with about fifteen different crews before he became their chaplain. As chaplain, he would accompany the crews on their calls, spending time with them and even being invited into their homes. He says it was such rewarding work and he credits it for doubling his church attendance. "Even if it wasn't the firemen who came to my church, they were in the community and they have friends and, when someone would say they were thinking of going to a church, I was mentioned because we have a relationship," he says.

Currently, Katona is priest-in-charge at St. Clement's Episcopal Church in Rancho Cordova in the Diocese of Northern California. Because the church was on a busy street, he decided to stand outside and wave at the cars passing by while he held different signs like "Free Grace," "Free Coffee," "This is a Sign." He tells me that twelve or fifteen people have started attending the church within the last year specifically because they saw him holding a sign on the side of the road. He says people love humor and it draws attention to the church. He says we could have flashing lights outside our church but when there's a person out there waving and making eye contact, it makes a difference.

Being in the community and building relationships is what Katona finds most important in ministry. When people visit the church, he tries to make a connection, looking for ways to see them again to start a relationship. For example, because many people who baptize their children may never go back to church, Katona offers to take some of the water in which the child was baptized and bless the family's home. He says he tries to make it a social visit and not only a blessing. He jokes that the main thing is to get into people's homes and then try to figure out what's the next thing you can invite yourself to in order to continue building the relationship. He encourages the parents of the baptized children to turn the event into a party and invite friends, neighbors, and family for the blessing. There, he makes conversation, starts relationships, and, with his love and enthusiasm, shares Jesus.

My dad has always modeled the importance of being outside of the church to build community, begin relationships, and evangelize. He would go around the community and get to know all the businesses and people he encountered. He and my mom (and us when the rest of the family was there) would often eat in the neighborhood restaurants, patronize the local businesses, and use the neighborhood mechanics even though they didn't live in the church's neighborhood. Papi is also part of the Police and Clergy Alliance, another way he established and bridged relationships and helped the community, particularly in an area with gang and other criminal activity.

My brother, Alex, a church planter, is also a big part of his community in Manor, Texas, where he has joined the Lions Club. He is well known in the area because he supports local businesses and volunteers at the local elementary school. As a church planter he understands that relationship building is the foundation for the future of his congregation.

It is so important for people to know that there is a church in their neighborhood, and especially a pastor and a community who are willing to walk the difficult life and faith walk with them. It is important for people to know that there is a God who loves them enough to send people who will speak with them, sharing the good news. Being visible and active in the community is a great first step to establishing respectful relationships and sharing the love of Jesus.

When you establish respectful relationships with the community, people know where to go when there is an emergency, a need for spiritual direction, or when they want to worship on a Sunday morning. When people see local pastors and parishioners around the neighborhood or even on television, trust is being established. Why would the television station know about you? Because pastors and members of the parish are also part of community engagement. If you are willing, you can be present at rallies, marches, and interfaith activities that benefit the neighborhood, helping build trust and relationships.

Part of starting respectful relationships is being welcoming. I have visited many churches throughout my life. When I go to a church that is welcoming, I want to return. This gives me and the church an opportunity to develop a respectful relationship. I want to see what else there is and what I may be missing out on.

Welcoming churches expect visitors because members are inviting people to come to their church all the time. Members of these welcoming churches are trained to recognize visitors. When they have a visitor, they treat them like a special guest, making them feel comfortable and answering any questions. I have seen ushers or other volunteers sit with visitors to help them with the liturgy and anything else the visitor may need. These volunteers also take the time to have short, meaningful conversations with visitors and may invite the visitors to share their contact information to continue with the conversation.

What does welcoming and initiating a respectful relationship look like with visitors? It looks like deep listening to people whom we have just met. It looks like smiles and handshakes and comments like "Come to coffee hour with us, please," and "We are so glad you are here!" There is a give-and-take, and everyone feels heard and ready to do it again. Welcoming churches have an established checklist or strategy for follow-up that will continue the relationship building.

People are social beings and so building relationships is not impossible, but it takes time. I have noticed that I have many friends who are involved politically. They organize parties where people can register to vote. They organize phone banks, making calls to ask for votes and even money. They support the candidate they believe will lead best and then they devote their time, energy, money, and talent. Does this sound familiar? I have also seen my friends canvass their neighborhood, sharing pamphlets, holding conversations with anyone who is curious or has questions. And, this includes my introverted, shy friends.

Imagine if we treated ministry like that. Imagine if we organized ourselves and went through our church neighborhood to tell people that Jesus loves them. Imagine what a difference it might make in someone's life. Imagine the impact your church could have. Of course, there would be people who would decline and that's fine. There would also be people who attend other churches or are part of other religions, but wouldn't it be amazing to have a conversation with them and ask them to keep you in their thoughts and prayers because you are all doing the work of God? This could be part of your prayer walk (see activities at the end of this chapter).

On Good Friday, San Mateo parish in Houston would take to the streets with songs, a live passion play, and lots of people sharing the good news. We went around the neighborhood, stopping to mark the Stations of the Cross. People from the houses and apartments would come outside to see what was going on. Members of the congregation were there to hand out information about God and our church. People were trained to pray with and for others, as needed. It was always touching when people would offer to carry Jesus's cross for a few blocks.

The respectful relationships my father had built with the police and neighborhood leadership around our church made much of this possible. My dad would visit all the police departments and other governmental bodies around the church to introduce himself, offer to pray for and with them, and offer our church when there was an emergency or a community need. He formed relationships with the schools and anyone he could around the church, and people often supported us, even if they did not attend our church.

Ashes to Go is a multidenominational practice of taking ashes to the streets on Ash Wednesday, offering prayers and the sign of the cross to any and all. Taking such a visible sign of faith to the streets makes it accessible and welcoming to everyone. This form of evangelism takes the church outside, where it truly belongs. Pastors and laypeople get to offer a prayer, a blessing, the ashes, and love to people who may not be able to attend a service or who have never been inside a church. I advise churches to offer something in writing or digitally for the people whom they have contact with—a business card-sized church advertisement, a prayer with the church's name and contact information on it, or a social media address for connection. Ashes to Go can be an opportunity to form relationships, even if they only last a few seconds or minutes. When we can share Jesus in a way that allows people to partake, even in a rushed moment, it is evangelism and relationship building. "Remember that you are dust, and to dust you shall return" provides a moment of touch, faith-sharing, and connection. I have seen many people crying as they approach an Ashes to Go station in the street. We are called to take Jesus to the streets, offering those unexpected encounters. We must take any opportunity to bring the love of Jesus to people where they are.

There are some who argue that Ashes to Go is not evangelism because there is no follow-up. I am always reminded of the parable of the sower when people say this: the parable reminds us that we sow the seed, God does the rest. Who are we to question who God wants to touch? If the chance for follow-up seems important, ask for people's information to keep in touch, pass out a positive message that includes your service times and contact information, including social media, or find another creative way to establish a follow-up. Know, however, that whether on the street or inside the church walls, God will continue to do what God wants to do.

There are many opportunities for us Christians to start respectful relationships with people in our neighborhood and around our church. Here are some ideas for every month of the year. What will make them unique is adding your neighborhood's or your church's culture and traditions to each suggestion.

January: New Year's resolution or vision board party. This can be done in the church or in a parishioner's home. You provide the snacks and place and ask people to bring materials.

February: Friendship or love game night. Don't call it a couple's date or anything that will limit participation. Invite people to come celebrate the love month by playing games— from board games to an obstacle course outside (weather permitting!) and everything in between. Have something for all ages and athletic abilities. The purpose is to build relationships.

March: St. Patrick's Day sing-along or hymn sing. Invite people to have green beer (or a green drink) and snacks as you sing hymns or songs that are popular in your congregation.

April: "Love Mother Earth" for Earth Day. Plan a community event filled with earth-friendly activities like planting flowers, starting a community garden, or cleaning up the beach. The whole month can be dedicated to loving Mother Earth.

May: Memorial Day celebration. Invite people to celebrate and honor those who gave the ultimate gift for our freedom. Reach out to the local armed forces recruitment office to see if someone could lead a workshop on the realities of being in a military family.

June: Water day. Invite everyone to a beach or a pool, or have a bunch of water games on the church's grounds (water balloons, water slide, car wash). Serve plenty of lemonade and fruit.

July: Independence picnic. Have everyone bring their own picnic baskets and blankets; you provide the entertainment, refreshments, and fireworks (if legal in your area).

August: Back-to-school backpack blessing. Invite students (any grade, any age) to bring their backpacks for a blessing during worship. Have backpack tags or key chains with a positive message or Bible verse to attach to people's backpacks, and a few gifts for inside the backpacks, like pencils or sticky notes. Also, print out the backpack blessing for them to keep.

September: Labor Day. Invite people to come clean up, fix up the church, do odd jobs, or help with the monthly newsletter or social media presence. Provide snacks and drinks and other incentives, like a raffle.

October: Spooky Bible stories. Invite people to dress up like the scariest or creepiest Bible story characters (beheaded

John the Baptist, Eve's snake, Job at his worst). Then, have people try to guess who they are and share the Bible story about each character. Provide opportunities for people to participate in non-spooky activities.

November: Thanksgiving month. Plan several activities around thanksgiving and the community. Hold a community Thanksgiving dinner or lunch on a day other than Thanksgiving Day so people can attend. Start a Thanksgiving Day food-to-go tradition and feed day workers or people on the streets.

December: Make an Advent wreath/calendar. Invite people to come to the church or a parishioner's home to make Advent wreaths or calendars. You provide the materials and hot cocoa and ask people to bring cookies.

When I worked at Christ Church Cathedral in Houston, I started *Noche Familiar* or Family Night. These were regular events when families (and singles) got together and had a night of hands-on projects. Everyone helped with the family project—advent calendar, family altar, and so on—and there was singing, Bible study, sharing, and food. The best part was that people brought their family and neighbors. Even those who did not attend our cathedral on Sunday or other days always came back for *Noche Familiar*.

Posadas is another way to bring people together to form respectful relationships. *Posadas* is a nine-day journey toward Christmas. It is a re-creation of the experience Joseph and Mary had when they were looking for a place for Mary to give birth, for *posada* (a place to stay). During this fun event, there are two groups of people: those who are inside, the innkeepers, and those who join Mary and Joseph, *los peregrinos* (pilgrims), outside. There are songs that people sing as they retell the story of Mary and Joseph looking for a place to rest and have their child.

At the end, the innkeepers open the door and Mary and Joseph, along with the pilgrims, come inside. There is usually hot cocoa and *pan dulce*, sweet bread, but some people prepare a full meal. A great tradition is to have eight *posadas* at people's homes and the last one at the church. As groups move from one home to the next, the crowd should grow, as each home's hosts and guests join the procession.

A *posada* can also be held outside of the church so passersby can see and join in. As you work toward creating this new tradition, remember the team building in preparation for holding a *posada* is part of the work of respectful relationships. Starting something new means that there isn't "the way we've always done it." New folks, long-standing members—everyone has an equal stake in the process. Have at least one pre-*posada* dinner or coffee get-together to plan the event, including discussing how to invite people outside the church to attend and what everyone can do to deepen relationships in their community.

Although we will talk more deeply about this in chapter 4, Authenticity, it is important to remember that celebrations such as these are not an opportunity to appropriate someone's culture. *Posadas* and other cultural celebrations like *Día de Muertos* are very important to people from different countries and cultures. If you have someone from that culture within your church, please remember to include them in the planning. I think *posadas* are a great way to foster community building, but I do not recommend them for places where there are no *gente Latina* who could lead this celebration. In respectful relationship building, we must remember that we are providing the space for the people outside our walls to feel welcome and included. If there are people around your church who have different cultural celebrations, including those in the life of the church is important and can be a bridge, but only if done with the guidance and support of someone who is part of that culture.

Besides fostering respectful relationships with people who are outside of your walls, have you made an effort to build relationships with people in your congregation or organization? It is not always easy. Developing new programs or groups is one way, but not the only way.

How can we start having conversations with our churchgoers that will help us strengthen our relationships? We must have them because that is what Jesus did as he commanded us to love each other. When we get to know those within our parish better, we can get to know those outside better. Respectful relationships foster additional respectful relationships. It's like the parable of the talents: God has given us gifts and they can be multiplied.

There are many ways to encourage conversations. One is actually in the middle of the service. Yes, this may seem disruptive or odd, but it is probably the time most people are together. As part of the sermon or announcements, post a question and have people share their responses with a partner or in groups of three. Another way to encourage conversations is to make intentional times for it—during Sunday school, during the week at Bible study, during coffee hour. Post questions on your social media page and ask people to respond to them, have ice-breaker games, create spaces where people can do crafts or other activities where conversations will organically happen. If the leadership is on board, the rest of the congregation will follow. Encourage the vestry and other key leaders to speak with a different person each Sunday and train greeters to introduce people who may have things in common (new parents, children in college, similar jobs) during coffee hour.

What does a liturgy that revolves around respectful relationships look like? It looks like a service that openly includes everyone who is part of your community. This not only means the people presently inside the church community, but the community outside the church as well. Because we are building community with our neighborhood by being part of the activities around it, we will be able to provide a variety of spiritual experiences. When we have respectful relationships and include diverse groups of people in decision-making, we will know more of what our neighbors need and want. Do you know the saying "when you have much, build a longer table"? As we know more about our neighbors, our invitations are more genuine and we open our church to a bigger altar—a table that holds wheelchairs and high chairs, with multiple languages spoken up and down its length. People who visit our churches will hopefully see themselves as they see God in our worship space, our liturgy, music, and prayers.

Westerners and Europeans made church—especially our beloved Episcopal Church—very "white," "Anglo," "English-centered." As we create a space where God is truly seen, it may need to look very different—many colors, many languages, many styles of art and music, etc. People of color are not visible—our buildings are filled with white icons, instruments from other cultures have been silenced by organ-heavy music. Liturgical design must always take into consideration who may be walking through the door.

When we are forming respectful relationships, we will notice our growing curiosity and openness; we may find ourselves incorporating new traditions in our own homes. That is definitely one way of celebrating new relationships. Think back to when you met your favorite people or best friends. When we first met and started getting to know each other, everything was new. Everything was interesting and we wanted to celebrate and experience everything with them. If they were from a different city or part of town, we wanted to know what that was like. We wanted to know about siblings or parents or how they grew up. Part of that is the search for common ground.

Common ground is important in establishing a relationship. Humans long to be connected and part of that connectivity lies in things we can share and have in common. We all want to feel appreciated and heard. Part of getting to common ground with others is by deeply listening, appreciating what they are saying. How can we get to this point with people who live in our communities but with whom we may have little in common? You won't know until you communicate. As soon as you start speaking with someone, you may find many things you hold in common. Remember that as you are establishing respectful relationships with people, they may also feel awkward or a little lost. Common ground helps communication, which leads to trust, and that trust is what we ultimately hope we can share.

When we are starting our respectful relationships and establishing trust, we must focus on the other person. Of course, you must share with them so they will also get to know you and feel the connection, but your goal is to have a respectful relationship with them, which means expressing interest in them rather than talking about yourself. As you both build trust, you may form a friendship. When this happens, it is easier to speak about more difficult topics, like faith.

One thing to note is that we must know who we are before we can truly get to know others. There are some who thrive in talking with others and there are some of us who would rather sit alone and smile as people walk by. As we are establishing respectful relationships because we are sharing the good news, it may be difficult. Don't pretend you are someone you're not. It is always a good thing to know what your needs are (space, quiet, time to decompress) if you are going to join your church's welcoming or canvassing team. If you know that you are more of a shy introvert, you may need to find other ways to form the respectful relationships that lead people to deep conversations.

Deep conversations lead people to sharing their story: we call this evangelism. For that to happen, of course, we must be in a place of safety. I am a very curious person, and tend to ask questions. This annoys some and others love it. Join me in finding a balance between being curious, wanting to get to know someone, and meddling. People want to be heard and not feel that whatever they say will be shared with other people.

Respectful relationships with people who are already in your congregation can be fostered by providing an opportunity for folks in the pews to share during the sermon. People don't often talk during the service, so it may be awkward at first, but this is a great way to connect and share a story. You may also want to invite people to share a "testimony" about what God is doing in their life. This may also be a little scary at first, but people become more comfortable as they are speaking and feel others sympathizing with them. The point is to help people feel connected with each other and form relationships.

When I was teaching, one of the best ways for students to retain new information was to have them share what they had learned or experienced. They felt empowered. Many times teachers don't get to talk to all their students in a day, so for them to share with each other helps each student feel heard as they process something new. Similarly, talking to others at church offers us an opportunity to listen to another's point of view.

One way some people show respect in developing relationships with those who speak other languages is to learn another language. I know people, including several Episcopal priests and bishops, who take intensive Spanish courses in Latin America for their work with *la gente Latina* in the United States. Immersion courses are great and they show commitment to learning a language other than your own. That is a great start. However, along with immersion into the language, it is important to be immersed into the culture, and that is best developed through relationships with individuals. I have met people who, as they are learning a new language, will interrupt native speakers because of their excitement about what they're learning. When we are learning, it is important to listen to our teachers (in the broadest sense of the word) first and then speak or comment or insert our opinions. When we do this, we show respect and humility.

Being respectful means giving the other person all the room to share what they have to teach. Think of times when you have been getting to know someone of another culture: What made it a good or bad experience? When another person is deeply listening to us, people of color, we feel heard. The other person is not thinking of what to say next but is authentically connecting with us. It is such a joy to hear someone say "tell me more" instead of "I know a person who looks just like you" or "I have a Hispanic friend." When people are listening, all of us feel valued and want to share more.

Another way to show respect in a relationship is remembering what people told us. There is nothing more beautiful than seeing a person after some time and noticing that they remembered our name and something about our life. When we talk about having respectful relationships in a church setting, we are talking about getting to a point in the relationship to share about Jesus. Although we may evangelize to gain more members for our churches, we are first and foremost evangelizing so people can come to Jesus. We hope they will see Jesus in our congregation and join us, but that isn't our primary goal. The foundation of a respectful relationship may include directing our new friends to a spiritual home that may not be ours.

Respectful relationships that don't seem forced or fake may best start with the church neighborhood. If your church is not in a neighborhood, then start with your own neighborhood, or that of someone from your parish who may live closer to the church. It is important for a neighborhood to have a church. Neighborhoods change as people move out and others move in. It's a great natural, unforced opportunity for respectful relationships. A neighborhood church that is changing can pose some challenges for the old guard, but, if they are committed to serving the community, the discomfort is not insurmountable. Respectful relationships make the difficult work of sharing power and influence with new neighbors and new parishioners possible.

Preparation is key. This can happen through formation classes, through sermons, through one-on-one conversations. The way forward will depend on the size of the congregation, the leadership, and the specifics of the situation. Before opening ourselves to new respectful relationships, we must respect the relationships we have made throughout the years and those who have chosen to remain in the church even when others have left. Just as when a new member of the family is entering our home, we must prepare the people who were there before for the new arrival.

With new children, we usually have a "gestation period" to share the great news with the older siblings and the larger family. Similarly, when we are hoping to start a new effort to bring more people from our community into our church, we must share that with the rest of the church family to help them prepare and understand. As with older siblings, sometimes even when we have done everything possible for them to understand what to expect, there are still plenty of surprises and people can react in the most unexpected ways.

Although our approach needs to be positive, we must also address what could go wrong. People need time to process that there are changes coming to their congregation, their church family, and the leadership must be prepared to answer questions and to be questioned. We must be prepared to help both the established congregation and the new possible members to come together and share the space by having prayer, Bible study, and opportunities to ask questions.

I have a friend who was visited by two leaders as part of a nearby church's canvassing excursion. He was very grateful for the visit because he had been asking God for a sign that God still cared. The persons were very warm, respectful, and seemed caring. They told my friend about their church and had a brief conversation about faith. They told him that anyone was welcome at the church and that they would be looking for him. They also gave him the church phone number and their personal e-mail addresses. They prayed with my friend, who felt so happy and at peace after the visit.

He e-mailed the two to thank them for the prayer and for the visit. They both e-mailed back, one almost instantly. The person who responded almost instantly kept writing to my friend. My friend felt a little odd about it but thought the person was just being friendly. After some texts after 10 p.m., he was anxious. At first, the person wasn't saying anything inappropriate or damaging, it was just odd that they kept writing. My friend stopped responding after the third or fourth text and after about an hour, the individual who prayed over my friend, who told him about Jesus and God's love, who invited him to come to church, asked, "Why are you ignoring me?" My friend did not know what to do. He had a minor anxiety attack.

He started thinking that they knew where he lived. They knew he lived alone. After about another hour the person wrote yet again, "OK. I GUESS I AM BOTHERING YOU. I WILL STOP NOW!" My friend blocked them and never went to that church. Thankfully, the individual did not go to my friend's house again, but it left my friend with a bad impression about church. He has yet to visit a church near him. That happened almost ten years ago.

We have to remember that people who are starting these relationships with us may not know Jesus. We may be the only Jesus they have ever encountered. What would Jesus do? That may have become a cheesy phrase but it is accurate. Would Jesus harass a new friend? Would Jesus stalk them? Would Jesus say offensive things? Would Jesus overstep or be rude? The answer to all those questions is no. Jesus would meet them where they were. He would invite them to a deeper relationship, without forcing himself on them.

There is nothing more annoying or off-putting than overly eager or desperate Christians trying to bring people to Christ or their church. People can sense that desperation. It is great to be received warmly when you enter a church, but it is not welcoming to be gawked at or paraded around. There may be a fine line between creepiness and genuine excitement about someone coming to church. I like to remind people how we act when we are dating. When we start dating others, we get turned off by desperate people, or people who seem creepy or like stalkers. This is like dating. When someone new comes through your doors, relax. Be excited and happy but not to the point of scaring someone away.

How might you begin the process of becoming REAL? Where are the opportunities for developing respectful relationships within your parish and among those who live in the neighborhood? Here are some ways to "just begin."

Activities

One-mile prayer walk

Alone or with a group (it is usually better to walk with a group, especially if you are an introvert, and during the day), walk around your church neighborhood using a one-mile radius (more or less depending on your own situation; you may need to get permission from the city for this). This walk could take more than one day depending on its length and the number of stops you plan. Stop at important landmarks like a school or a juvenile detention center. Engage with whoever is around the landmark (unless otherwise indicated). It is important to make connections during this prayer walk so be prepared. Take small cards to pass out with the church's information, the name of a contact person who can answer their questions or can pray with and for them, and a Bible verse and inspirational quote.

For your prayer walk create a sheet with prayers from various sources including the Book of Common Prayer, and stop along the way to pray. You may want to wear matching T-shirts, if you're going as a group, that say what church you are representing so you can be easily identified.

As you walk, ask the following questions and write down everything you see and experience:

What kind of businesses do you see (you could have a tally sheet for restaurants, laundromats, car wash places, and so on)? What kind of services are provided? Are there young families? Are there a lot of youth and children? Are there schools, daycares, other educationally focused entities? Are the signs in other languages or just in English? Are there places where people could congregate, like a park or a public garden? Can people safely walk this radius? Are there homeless people or people who look like they may be in distress?

After your walk, go back to your church and debrief as a group. You can ask: Does your church reflect what you saw in your prayer walk? Does your church have presence in its surroundings? Are there people volunteering at the schools or shelters that surround your church buildings? Is your neighborhood thriving but your church dying? What did you notice that surprised you? Do those who attend your church look like the people you saw around your neighborhood?

You may want to do another prayer walk with other people from your church. You can use the data collected in the prayer walk or walks to propel you into the ministry you are called to.

Reflective listening

In pairs, practice listening for one to two minutes, and then be the other person's "mirror" and paraphrase what was shared. Switch.

Listening session

Invite people with whom you want to develop relationships to come to a listening session. During your time together, the goal is truly to listen to whatever your new friends and neighbors want to share. However, do not make it uncomfortable or put them on the spot by expecting your guests to do all the work. As hosts, provide starter questions and have a plan if they are not prepared to share. Do all you can to create a comfortable, inviting space for conversation rather than interrogation.

Bible or book study

During this time of relationship building, one great way to start is by having a Bible or book study. You might want to start with Proverbs or the Psalms or choose an inspirational book. Decide how often you will meet—once a week or once every other week would be best so you can continue to get to know each other. Then, choose the format you will use. There are different ways to hold a Bible study: one is called the African Bible study method, another is called *Lectio Divina*. A simple way is to open with a prayer, read a chapter or a section of a book, then discuss. There is no wrong way to study the Bible because the purpose is to get to know the scripture and get to know each other.

Neighborhood resource map

This is a great relationship-building activity for your congregation. Share the places around the church that you found on your one-mile prayer walk. Create a handout, craft a poster large enough to set up on an easel, or design a digital document that the group can access. Add to the list at meetings as others mention locations. With this list, make a large map to post prominently on the wall. Include the places where the church community spends their time. Encourage the parish leadership, lay and ordained, to visit those places that are identified as important for the community.

Because part of being in relationship is meeting people where they are, consult your neighborhood resource map often. For example, if you are hoping to get more young families involved in your church or program, a good place to meet them would be at a child-friendly establishment near your church, like a fast-food restaurant or diner, a daycare center, or a baby or toy store.

Yearbooks

Invite people to come for a festive event. When folks arrive, provide nametags and ask everyone to write their name and what year they started attending the church. After initial ice breakers, gather everyone into decade groups. For example, if Monica started attending in 2009 and Mildred started in 2001, they might be in a 2000–2010 group. Pose questions for each group to consider, like, "What was the most memorable thing that happened during your decade?" or "If you could go back, what would you change?" For the newest members or visitors, ask questions about their hopes for the church and their needs. Invite people to share with the larger group.

Music

Music is a very important part of community building and our faith. One way to get people talking about music and their musical preferences is to have a talent show where people can offer their musical talents. Another is to have a sing-along where people can choose from a list of well-known songs (not necessarily hymns). An activity that worked well in different churches I attended was to ask people what songs they like. For example, I have created a survey in the past where people can share their top three "churchy" songs and their top three "non-churchy" songs. We will do this during the offertory: "Everyone with a smartphone, please use the QR code or the short link to go to the survey and fill it out." Or, if people do not have smartphones, then we pass out slips of paper. They can write their name if they like. We have choir members walking around just in case someone knows the songs they love but can't remember the names. This is a great way to get to know each other. You can also take about five minutes to ask people to share what they wrote with their neighbor. It is rare that we get to talk during church time, so it may be a little awkward at first. When people start opening up, it becomes a joyful noise. To get everyone back on track, sing one of your favorite songs that people know or can learn easily.

Technology

Create a group text (get permission or include parents if this will be used with young people) or Slack page to stay connected with those with whom you are developing relationships. This is to foster communication and to share information easily. Use this text group or page to encourage people in their daily walk by sharing a Bible verse or an inspirational quote. You can also send reminders about the upcoming activities at church.

Look at the church's social media pages. Do you have pictures of people of all ages, ethnicities, abilities, and so on? What about your own social media pages? Are you intentionally engaging with people unlike yourself? Are you and your parish fostering relationships that go beyond your "norm"?

Capítulo 2: Relaciones respetuosas

A lo largo de mi vida, he visto la importancia de las relaciones. Cuando tenía cuatro años, mi familia se mudó de nuestro país de origen, Perú, a Guatemala, donde mi papi iba a asistir al seminario. No teníamos familiares ni amigos en Guatemala y nuestra relación como familia se fortaleció mucho al tener que depender el uno del otro. Construir relaciones requiere tiempo, energía, esfuerzo e intencionalidad. Construir relaciones respetuosas es un trabajo duro y muy gratificante.

Las personas me dicen que les gustaría más jóvenes, niños, personas diversas, personas multilingües en sus organizaciones o iglesias. Cuando pregunto por qué, la respuesta a menudo revela las creencias y el compromiso detrás del comentario. Si has dicho: "Me gustaría tener más jóvenes en mi iglesia," o algo así, medita sobre el "porqué". ¿Dios ha puesto ese grupo en tu corazón por alguna razón? ¿Has visto alrededor de tu vecindario y has sentido que ese grupo no está siendo atendido? Si tu respuesta no tiene nada que ver con crecer en el Espíritu de Dios y compartir el amor de Jesús con los demás, necesitas pensar un poco más.

Como líderes, nuestro trabajo, después de evangelizar, es estar presentes y visibles en nuestras comunidades. Sugiero que los líderes hagan una caminata de oración a solas o con un grupo alrededor de su iglesia, organización u hogar. En otras palabras, mientras caminas, medita en un versículo bíblico o en oraciones (el Libro de Oración Común tiene varias). También puedes detenerte en las esquinas y orar en voz alta o cantar un himno. Mientras caminas y oras, anota todo lo que ves. ¿Qué tipo de servicios hay en el vecindario? ¿Hay muchos jóvenes y niños? ¿Hay escuelas, guarderías, otras entidades enfocadas en la educación? ¿Hay lugares donde las personas pueden congregarse, como un parque o un jardín público?

Una vez que terminas tu caminata de oración, usa tus datos para ver cuál es el grupo que necesita tu ministerio. Comienza a establecer relaciones respetuosas con las personas que componen ese grupo.

El primer paso que puedes dar cuando quieres comenzar una relación con un grupo de personas (jóvenes, familias, diferentes grupos étnicos, etc.) es ir a donde ellos están. Si quieres construir relaciones con los jóvenes, comienza donde pasan la mayor cantidad de tiempo: la escuela. ¿Hay una escuela secundaria o preparatoria cerca? ¿Hay maestros de secundaria o preparatoria en tu congregación? Si la respuesta es sí a cualquiera de estas interrogantes, ¡genial! Puedes comenzar a construir esas relaciones presentándote, iniciando la conversación con personas que forman parte de esa comunidad o que pueden llevarte a ellas.

Las relaciones toman tiempo y, cuando quieres construir relaciones con personas que aún no están en tu organización o iglesia, puede ser más difícil comenzarlas orgánicamente. Debes presentarte ante la gente para que comiencen a confiar en ti. Debes estar realmente interesado/a en lo que necesitan y les gusta. ¿Cómo puedes descubrir sus deseos o necesidades? Pregúntales. No pienses que sabes cuáles son sus necesidades.

A medida que vas conociendo a las personas y desarrollando una relación respetuosa, escucha activamente. Permíteles hacer preguntas y dales tanta información, recursos, y dirección como sea necesario, cuando te lo pidan.

Es importante recordar que establecer relaciones respetuosas como parte del evangelismo no es para que las personas vayan a tu iglesia, sino para mostrarles el amor de Dios. Muchas personas pueden reconocer cuando alguien está siendo falso, así que tenlo en cuenta cuando estés ofreciendo tu amistad respetuosa.

Ofrece capacitación a tu congregación sobre cómo evangelizar y cómo comenzar una relación respetuosa. Es útil para aquellos que participan en estas oportunidades de construir relaciones respetuosas estar preparados con información básica sobre su organización o iglesia, denominación, sus creencias y cómo establecer buenas conversaciones.

Las personas que tienen relaciones respetuosas saben que no todos vamos a pensar lo mismo o a estar de acuerdo todo el tiempo. Todos venimos con diferentes experiencias, culturas y creencias. Es por eso que cuando comenzamos estas relaciones respetuosas, es esencial escuchar. Debemos crear espacios para la comunicación y las conversaciones. Debemos buscar y proveer oportunidades para construir estas relaciones en nuestras comunidades.

Mi papi, un sacerdote episcopal retirado que fue el primer rector de la primera parroquia totalmente latina y autosuficiente en los Estados Unidos, entró a la Iglesia a través de una relación respetuosa. Se escapó de casa cuando era un niño por abuso físico. Estuvo sin hogar y vivió en las calles de Lima. Cuando era un adolescente, comenzó a trabajar para una familia cristiana que lo amó. Siempre lo invitaban a ir a la iglesia con ellos y él siempre decía que no. Sin embargo, a través de esa relación, porque la familia satisfizo sus necesidades de comida, vivienda y trabajo, finalmente accedió a asistir a la iglesia. Cuando fue a la iglesia con la familia, su vida cambió. No lo obligaron a asistir, no lo amenazaron, lo invitaron, después de haber establecido una relación respetuosa con él.

Después de un tiempo, mi papi sintió el llamado al ministerio y fue a la universidad bíblica donde conoció a mi mami. Establecieron, o como decimos los episcopales en los Estados Unidos, plantaron algunas iglesias en Perú y luego mi papi fue al seminario en Guatemala. Después de graduarse decidió aceptar una invitación para ser pastor en los Estados Unidos. Mientras era pastor de la Iglesia Alianza Cristiana y Misionera en el valle del Río Grande de Texas, asistió a una conferencia ecuménica de Evangelismo Explosivo en Nueva York. Allí conoció a Hugo

Pina, un obispo episcopal. Años más tarde, mi papi repartía pizzas (no ganaba suficiente dinero como pastor) cuando le robaron, golpearon y dejaron por muerto. En el hospital, llamó a su pastor, quien le dijo que lo llamara cuando volviera a casa. Mi papá estaba triste y se sentía solo. Recordó haber conocido a este obispo años antes y que vivía en Houston. Mi papi encontró la tarjeta del obispo Pina y le llamó, quien respondió que iría tan pronto como pudiera.

Mi papi siempre recuerda haber visto al obispo Pina corriendo a su habitación con su hermoso atuendo episcopal. Comenzaron esa relación años antes, sin saber que Dios los volvería a unir en esta trágica situación. Mi papi comenzó a ayudar al obispo Pina en San Mateo con la limpieza; luego comenzó a ayudar con la música y el estudio bíblico. Un día, el obispo Pina le dijo a mi papi: "Alejandro, Dios te ha llamado para entregar las buenas nuevas, no para entregar pizza", y así comenzó la travesía de mi papi en la Iglesia Episcopal. Todo por una relación respetuosa que comenzó en una conferencia y que se consolidó gracias a que el obispo Pina sintió que era importante estar presente donde estaba mi papi.

Hay gente sufriendo en todo el mundo. Necesitan que les llevemos a Jesús donde ellos se encuentran. Necesitan relaciones arraigadas en el respeto, la paciencia, el amor y el compromiso. Necesitan relaciones transformadoras. Ni puedo imaginar lo que hubiera pasado si el obispo Pina no hubiera ido a ver a mi papi. Fue la relación respetuosa que el Obispo Pina y mi papi construyeron lo que les ayudó a ambos a imaginar un futuro en el que mi papi, un pastor evangélico, pudiera dirigir una comunidad episcopal construida por inmigrantes católicos romanos.

Parte de establecer relaciones con las personas es simplemente salir de nuestras iglesias. Para llevar las buenas nuevas, tenemos que tomar el primer paso de levantarnos, salir e involucrarnos con las personas a nuestro alrededor.

Van a haber personas que solo van a ir a la iglesia porque necesitan una quinceañera, un bautismo, una bendición. Por eso es tan importante que estemos listos para recibirles y decirles que Dios les ama y que no hay nada más importante que establecer una relación con Dios. Tomemos cualquier oportunidad para bendecir a la gente que está buscando a Dios y recordarles que son importantes. Si están buscando un lugar donde tener su quinceañera, toma la oportunidad para incluir a la persona joven en tu ministerio juvenil. Si están buscando bautizar a su bebé, usa la oportunidad para invitarles a que se unan a su estudio bíblico para las familias. Tenemos que estar listos para recibir a personas de nuestro vecindario y comenzar a establecer una relación respetuosa. No nos preocupemos si las personas se van a quedar después de haber tenido la quinceañera, el bautismo o la primera comunión—probablemente no. Sólo preocupémonos por presentarles a Jesús y su amor a través de nosotros.

Como personas latinas, sabemos dar la bienvenida. Somos gente alegre y cariñosa. Pero también demos la bienvenida con nuestro tiempo, ayuda y tratemos de invitar a las personas de nuestro alrededor a la iglesia y hagamos seguimiento con ellas. Podemos salir al vecindario de casa en casa para presentarles a nuestra iglesia y para ver si necesitan ayuda y oración. No tiene que ser una visita larga ni complicada; sólo es para presentarse y para ofrecer una amistad respetuosa. Siempre lleva un folleto que tenga la información importante de tu iglesia incluyendo el horario y cómo se pueden comunicar con la iglesia. Si la persona no quiere abrir la puerta, no insistas. Si la persona va a otra iglesia pídele que ore por tu ministerio.

Cada Viernes Santo, la parroquia de San Mateo en Houston salía a la calle con cantos, el vía crucis dramatizado en vivo y mucha gente compartiendo las buenas nuevas. Dábamos la vuelta al vecindario parando para marcar las Estaciones de la Cruz. Las personas de las casas, negocios y apartamentos salían a ver qué estaba pasando. Los miembros de la congregación estaban listos para entregar información sobre Dios y nuestra iglesia y orar por las personas. Siempre era conmovedor ver cuando la gente se ofrecía para cargar la cruz de Jesús por unas pocas cuadras.

Otra tradición era Cenizas para llevar o para el camino (*Ashes to Go*). Mi papi caminaba por las calles el miércoles de ceniza solo o acompañado por un líder y daban cenizas y oraban por las personas en las calles, en los negocios y en lugares donde les invitaban. Siempre tenía un folleto o tarjeta para explicar lo que significaban las cenizas.

Algo que pueden hacer como iglesia para invitar a las personas de su vecindario es tener eventos especiales. Yo comencé la noche familiar en la catedral en Houston. La gente venía con sus familias; teníamos comida, música y manualidades. Era un tiempo para conocernos y para hacer algo juntos. Las Posadas pueden ser una manera de ir a las casas donde las personas que van a la iglesia pueden invitar a sus vecinos—algunos que tal vez no van a ninguna iglesia—para mostrarles el amor de Dios a través de cantos, historias y hasta comida. Yo he visto que hay varias iglesias que tienen una tamalada durante el tiempo de Navidad e invitan a personas de la comunidad para que vengan a comprar tamales y hasta a hacerlos juntos. Cualquier evento o fiesta que hagan, inviten a las personas de la vecindad para que conozcan a su iglesia o ministerio y así comiencen las relaciones respetuosas.

También es necesario que las personas en la iglesia tengan relaciones respetuosas. A veces vamos a la misma iglesia por años y no nos conocemos. Una manera de hacer amistad es teniendo conversaciones durante el servicio. Puede comenzar con una pregunta que van a responder durante la paz o después del sermón. Puede ser una pregunta sobre las lecturas, o sobre lo que está pasando en el mundo. También, cada persona de la junta parroquial o del comité del obispo puede hablar con diferentes personas cada domingo y así conocerlas mejor.

¿Cómo es una liturgia que gira en torno a las relaciones respetuosas? Es un servicio que incluye abiertamente a todos los que forman parte de la comunidad. No solo las personas actualmente dentro de la iglesia, sino también la comunidad fuera de la iglesia. Como estamos construyendo comunidad con nuestro vecindario, al tener varias actividades, podremos brindar una variedad de experiencias espirituales. Cuando tenemos relaciones respetuosas e incluimos diversos grupos de personas en la toma de decisiones, sabemos más de lo que nuestros vecinos necesitan y quieren. Primero Dios, las personas que visiten nuestras iglesias se verán a sí mismas en nuestro espacio de adoración, nuestra liturgia, música y oraciones porque las conocemos y las tenemos presente durante la planificación de ellas.

CHAPTER 3

Excellence

Do not worry, do not fear. I am your God, I'm always near.
Do not worry, do not fear. I am your God, I'm always,
I'm always here.

"Do Not Fear" / "No tengas miedo"
—text and tune by Sandra Montes

There are some people who cringe at the word "excellence" because they equate it with perfection, and there are some who thrive when given a challenge to better their approaches. We read in Philippians 4:8, "Finally, beloved, whatever is true, whatever is honorable, whatever is just, whatever is pure, whatever is pleasing, whatever is commendable, if there is any excellence and if there is anything worthy of praise, think about these things." This encourages all of us to keep excellence in mind.

There is nothing wrong with striving for perfection, as long as you are not harming yourself or others. What we must remember is to be gentle and patient with people who need to strive for perfection and with those who do not like to see life in those terms. We must do our best for the "people" we are called to serve. Those in the pews ten years ago, or even five, are not the same as the ones who are there today—even if they are the same people. People grow, and so must our programs, offerings, music, leaflets, and welcome.

For me, I don't mind the word "excellence" and feel that I have been striving for excellence for a long time. I am a bit concerned to use the word "perfect" because I was brought up to think that the only perfection is God. For some, the word "perfection," just like "excellence," carries negative, harmful, or even abusive memories.

For me, excellence looks like the hours I spend learning a new song. I do not like being unprepared. Because I cannot sight-read music, I must do my homework before any event where I am singing. Being committed to excellence can help us be ready for the unexpected.

My son, Ellis, sees excellence in this way:

On the first day that I went to visit Grace Episcopal Church in Houston, I felt like I was witnessing a community event, which was something I had not experienced so strongly in a church in quite a while. The readers, acolytes, musicians, congregants, and priests all gave energy to one another, and that energy was something I felt. I remember feeling like the readers were telling an important message just to me. They raised their heads and made eye contact while also relaying what God had to say to us that day. The music was played quite well, and the variety was quite inspiring. At the time, I knew very little about the congregation, but witnessing the music helped me understand the complicated history behind the congregation. In a song, I was able to hear the charismatic Christianity from the past of different musicians. I could hear the three different congregations that had merged over time to become Grace. I could hear the different colors, languages, races of people who all had a place at the table. I could hear the old and the young generations passing on a tradition and growing a culture together.

When I visit churches, I always notice the aesthetics. Not how expensive things are, but rather how much pride people are putting into their space. Maybe I am using "pride" incorrectly, but I am translating it from Spanish where it means that people are trying to show their best for anyone who comes into the space. I understand that we all have different definitions of what looks best, what is most polished, what is cluttered and what is holy mess, but basic things like cleanliness, organization, and creating a welcoming space are not expensive. What is a church community trying to convey to those who are attending for the first time?

Do you have a ramp for people who need it? Do you have handrails, if you have steps, for people to hold, especially when it's rainy or snowy? Do you have restrooms that are safe and accessible for all? Do you have seating that is easy to get to? Is communion delivered to people who cannot reach the altar? Do you have a team who take communion and hope to homebound people? Are services or sermons online for people to access easily? All of these have to do with mobility, and this has become especially important to me since my dad suffered a stroke. I must admit, even though mobility and accessibility were important to me for years, they have become even more so because I have a loved one who needs them. What better reminder that relationship with people of all walks of life is very important?

What does your service leaflet or bulletin look like? Does it include instructions? Are they easy to follow? I have visited churches where everything feels like a maze. The leaflet or bulletin does not explain how to navigate the liturgy. So, if you're new, especially if you're not from a liturgical tradition, following along is like an intricate salsa dance when all you can do is walk. Some churches have decided to use projection and not have any paper leaflets or bulletins or books. This makes everything easy for those of us who can see the projected screens but raises its own set of other issues.

Some churches may choose to hand out Books of Common Prayer, hymnals, bulletins, and/or lectionary readings as individuals walk into the worship space. If churches are committed to excellence, they will discuss what the best practice is for that church and will have a plan for visitors and newcomers; they will discuss how people who may not be able to see or move easily can navigate the service. In a church I served, we offered large-print leaflets, but often did not include the songs. It takes planning, time, ink, and paper if we are going to supply the entire service in one leaflet, but it is essential to have conversations about what is best for our particular setting if we are committed to excellence in our church. This is why it is important to have a variety of people with a variety of needs be part of decision-making. The team may not be able to provide for every possible need, but when there is diversity in a group, there is a bigger chance of capturing more viewpoints.

What does all that mean? When we are working toward excellence, a variety of people should be engaged in serving during the liturgy. For example, when I attend churches, I pay attention to who is reading, who is at the altar, who is greeting, etc. If you are hoping to attract more young people, you must have young people as part of the visible leadership. When you include youth in planning meetings, they will be able to tell you what they need. They will tell you if the pastor should wear sneakers instead of dress shoes (s/he shouldn't) or if the pastor should have more tattoos or piercings (not unless that is their style) or if the music needs a makeover (it probably does). If you hope to attract more young people, do you have formation classes or small groups for their ages with leaders who are trained and experienced with people of those ages? The best people to school you in what you need to attract more youth are youth.

When we are committed to excellence and want to attract young families and youth, we must have excellent offerings for them. All of them. We can't have a great youth program and neglect the children's Sunday school hour. We can't have great adult and parenting classes and neglect youth activities. None of this needs to have a huge dollar sign attached, but it must have commitment and effort.

Volunteer leaders and teachers will almost always need (and appreciate) training. Sometimes we keep long-term volunteers because they are beloved, have been in the role for many years, or out of fear that they will leave if we ask them to consider another ministry. That is not being excellent. That is being scared or set-tling for the familiar and habitual. As people who have respect-ful relationships with those in our congregation and as people committed to excellence, we should be able to ask someone to try another ministry when their gifts are not best used in their current ministry. Part of being a mature Christian is being able to speak truth in love and being able to accept, listen, and change or adjust.

For formation classes, teachers should have a training ses-sion at least once a semester. Purchase books and subscriptions to educator and formation magazines or websites that have activ-ities, suggestions, and ideas. Meet with your teachers at least once a quarter to talk about each liturgical season. Be prepared in advance for the upcoming feast days like Easter when attendance may swell. As leaders in the church, we must also be committed to people where they are and help them get where we pray for them to be—to a deeper relationship with Jesus. We, like Jesus did with us, must go and take the good news with us, in our hearts, minds, hands, feet, and lips. We must prepare ourselves in order to help others prepare. We must be formed before we can form others. It is so much better for people to learn from our example.

I have heard that we should accept anything when it is being done for God or at church. I agree and disagree. I have always believed that the best is what we need to give to God, not our leftovers or the gifts we may wish we had. When we are dis-cerning in prayer where God wants us to minister, we will be directed, and everything will fall into place.

As people committed to excellence, your congregation, including your newest members (or even visitors), may choose to take spiritual gift inventories. These can show where each one can use the unique gifts God has given. After taking the inventory as a congregation, however, be prepared to follow up with a concrete plan. For example, if my spiritual gifts inventory finds that I have a gift for teaching, but I want to evangelize (a gift low on my inventory), there should be someone on hand to help me see what my options could be and to answer my questions. Those who want to volunteer because they want to give back to God will volunteer. We mustn't be afraid to work with them to find the ministry that fits their inventory results.

How can we be excellent while participating in the regular church stuff like ushering, reading, singing, and so on? How can that truly help others see God's love and Jesus's invitation to come to him? Excellence is biblical—do everything as though it were for God. That certainly does not mean do everything mediocrely or halfway, but rather it means do everything with pride and as best as you can.

I can't imagine how tough it must be for some people to go into a church. I wonder what it is like when parents of small children attend your church for the first time. Has your church planned for that? If you are hoping to attract more families with young children, ask yourselves: What does your nursery or childcare space look like? What does your sanctuary look and sound like? Would a person with a baby feel awkward or nervous because everything is too quiet inside your church? Are there changing stations in the restrooms, and rocking chairs that allow the parent to care for their child and still enjoy being part of the service? Is there a designated area inside the sanctuary for children to sit and play with quiet toys? Are there bags of toys and Bible activities for the children who decide to stay in the "big" church? Does your pastor have a child's story or sermon? Does your church offer a children's chapel? Is there a special blessing over the children who attend?

If we are being excellent in our welcome to families with children, we may:

1. Have youth or families in leadership.

2. Have spaces for youth or families, especially those with small children or children who may need to move during worship.

3. Expect youth and families to visit and plan accordingly by providing nursery care, child-friendly bulletins, and soft toys and books within the worship space.

Look at all the things you already have in place to welcome children, youth, and their parents and celebrate that. Do not leave it there, however. Check at least once every six months to see what is working, what can be added (do you incorporate Godly Play and have trained facilitators?), what needs to change (are the rocking chairs dirty?), and what needs to improve (is the youth minister using outdated methods or curriculum?). That is what a church community devoted to excellence does.

When we are committed to excellence and we are hoping to attract young families, we make our church attractive for them. We will find teachers for Sunday school and great people for childcare. We will invest in toys, books, cribs, changing tables, a playground, Godly Play or other formation options, and other things that will help families feel welcome and comfortable. In excellent churches, we see spaces for the families, like rocking chairs and areas specifically designated for nursing moms, areas designated for quiet child play, and other amenities such as quiet sanctuary toy bags, great snacks, and a way for parents to comfortably leave their children in the daycare.

No matter who you are hoping to attract, if you are not working toward excellence with the programs, liturgy, music, and ministry God has called you into, you may not be ready for the rest of the harvest to arrive. First, take an inventory of your programs and activities and review what can be improved, let go, modified, and updated (see the activities at the end of this chapter). There are many excuses not to be excellent in church settings—time, lack of volunteers, no funds—but none of them are valid when we think about the mandate to love and share the good news.

When we hold events that we hope people who are not currently part of our worshiping community will attend, what are we doing to make sure people will feel comfortable and welcome? This is a great time to start with the respectful relationship's invitation to canvass your community and see who lives around your church. A simple short visit introducing yourself, your church, and your activity is perfect. Finish by asking if there is anything they would like you to pray for—either at that moment or during your prayers of the people—and pray. If they are receptive, great! If they go to another church, wonderful, ask them to pray for your church and let them know they are always welcome to visit. If they are not interested, be courteous—remember that they may someday need your services and it is better to have friendly neighbors than people who think you're not to be trusted. Create a short pamphlet for these visitors to take with them. Maybe it includes a poem or a short positive thought or anything that you think may give some comfort and joy. Include the church's contact information, the activity's time and date, and website or social media information.

I met a pastor who began a service in Spanish because many of the people who lived around his church were Spanish-speakers. He did not have access to the Book of Common Prayer in Spanish (*El Libro de Oración Común*) and he did not have the money to buy resources or to pay someone to translate their resources. So, with his poor Spanish, he translated what he could, typed it up, printed it, and made little booklets for their Sunday worship. The people in his congregation were excited and grateful because they could worship in Spanish and had some resources to help.

Years later, I visited them and they were still using the very worn booklets. Some of the booklets had been "updated" or "corrected" using blue or red ink. The congregation had grown, and yet the booklets had not. I spoke with the pastor and was able to get them free copies of *El Libro de Oración Común* and other resources. It is one thing to use whatever you have when you are first starting, knowing it is a starting point. If you have used the same PowerPoint presentation, the same booklet, the same songbook, the same anything for many years, however, and have not updated it, it is probably time to commit to being excellent and see what can be updated. This does not mean that you have to throw out resources or books or Bibles; it means that you must be aware of what you are giving the people who visit your community.

Part of my passion is showing excellence on social media or the internet. I have gone to many diocesan and church websites and have gotten lost or have not been able to find basic information. The most important thing is to update your website and social media presence often, especially during seasons like Easter and Christmas when people are most likely to look for a place to worship. When a website or social media platform is updated, uncluttered, user-friendly, and welcoming, people are more likely to want to visit the church it is representing.

Of similar importance is that your basic information—leadership, address, service times, contact information, and whom to contact for what—must be easily visible and shouldn't require a separate click to get to. If I have to click more than once or twice, I am going to leave your webpage and will go to another church on Sunday.

I encourage people to post pictures and videos of what their church is and what it hopes to be. (Follow best practices, know your parish or diocesan policies, and keep updated release forms, especially if posting images of children.) People have told me that they will attend a service depending on the photos they see. If they see people who look like them, smiling and obviously engaged, they are more likely to attend a service. This isn't to encourage the use of fake stock photos or posting several pictures of your one "diverse" person—rather, use images of what your church looks like, even if it is not diverse. Hopefully, one day soon it will be more diverse and you can also share that with the world.

A church that is working to be excellent is welcoming to visitors. This church has a vision and knows how to achieve her goals. This does not mean she is not scared or doesn't make mistakes. It means that the church is planning with a variety of people at the table who are committed to this vision of what they hope to be in the future. That future includes people from all walks of life and, hopefully, from their neighborhood and beyond.

Are you planning for the upcoming liturgical seasons? Do you have several resources available to consult as you choose music and various liturgical texts? Are you planning with a diverse team? If you want to be excellent, planning is important. You will be ready to make changes as they come instead of being surprised at the last minute when things don't go well. Part of planning and being excellent is explaining what the liturgical seasons are and what the colors associated with them signify. There are books and other resources available to help explain the liturgy, but wouldn't it be great if your church provided that—in video or print form—to its parishioners, created by parishioners?

I recommend planning at least three months in advance, especially when it comes to the selection of new music and liturgies. It is also a good idea to speak with other leaders who may be planning for the upcoming liturgical seasons or big feast days—those who work with children or youth, for example. Coordination and communication are key to excellence and to planning.

Planning well in advance also allows an opportunity to plan events that center around community-building and reaching out to those who are not part of your church. For example, make save-the-date fliers to pass out in the community as you prepare for Mardi Gras or Shrove Tuesday celebrations. As with any event, being able to invite the community in advance through fliers or social media will provide visibility as you work to connect with your community.

Over the years, as I have been invited to sing or to speak, I never know how many people will be present. Sometimes there are very few people and sometimes there are more. It is not easy to prepare for a few people sometimes. As I get older, I realize that execution may look different, but the preparation is usually the same, large group or small. I prepare for the audience, however big or small it may be. I want people to know that I am committed to them and that they are important. I want to know, for myself, that I will be prepared no matter the context in which I will be presenting. I am committed to excellence because of my commitment to being like Jesus, showing respect and love for people.

I keep talking about planning because being prepared is important when we are committed to excellence. For example, lectors, it is advisable to have a rotating list of people who will be reading on any given Sunday. This list should be created at least a month in advance and must be accurate and updated whenever there is a change or adjustment. Post this list prominently and send reminders via text, e-mail, snail mail, or social media. Lectors should also receive a copy of the reading one week in advance unless they asked for it sooner. Be available to go over the reading with anyone who wants to practice.

When children serve as lectors, you may want to select readings that are not too complicated and do not have very adult subject matter. Children may need to have their parents help them during the week, and if you notice there is a tricky word, let them know in advance. This is also helpful for people who read and speak other languages.

This same principle is applicable for all ministries. Always plan and prepare. This is what excellence is built on. Do you know the saying "perfect practice makes perfect"? As a musician, I understand this. If I have been practicing something incorrectly, I will learn it incorrectly and it will become a bad habit. However, if I am practicing correctly, then my offering will go well.

Planning is essential in working toward excellence in music. As you are getting to know people who may be new to your congregation, ask if there are songs that they love to sing or perform during different times of the year. I have discovered a lot of great Advent and Christmas music from around the world this way. If you plan for your church or choir to sing songs that may be new to them or in a different language, you must rehearse well in advance to learn the new songs well. There may not be a musical score available, so your choir may need extra time to learn the music. If you are planning to sing music in other languages (more on this in the next chapter), have a person who speaks the language available for rehearsals, if no one in the ensemble is a native or fluent speaker of that language. If no one is available, a recording of a native speaker singing the song is helpful. I have recorded many Spanish-language songs with a short tutorial for my friends' rehearsals throughout the years.

When we are doing things in an excellent way, we plan early enough to be able to use songs that may seem too difficult at first glance. I suggest introducing only one or two—if the songs are very simple—new songs every week. There is nothing wrong with introducing new music weeks or months before singing it as a congregational hymn, especially when we are doing things with excellence and diversity. I must admit that if I go to a church and see only one hymnal and no other resources or projection—making it possible to add another song on the spot—then my heart sinks because I think the music needs to be updated. When I see other hymnals or songbooks and a projection screen, I am excited to see what we will sing. Have I been surprised by the churches I felt were going to bore me with their music or disappointed by those I thought would be innovative? Of course. Updating our music resources, practicing, and taking risks with our congregation in mind is part of being excellent.

Many have found the Episcopal Church over the years because of its excellence in music, in preaching, and in liturgy. Although we may think that people come only for excellent classical or traditional liturgical music, we may be surprised to find that people will come for excellent music, period. There are ways to bring amazing non-Western traditional music to church, including classical music from other countries and cultures. When we decide we are going to strive for excellence, we bring excellence to everything we do, even when it is difficult or new.

If your church community is near a university or a music school, use them as a valuable resource. You may be able to offer space for concerts that involve students of the school who will then invite their friends and families. That is a great way to introduce Jesus without a sermon. Have beautiful postcards, business cards, or small pamphlets made that list service times, website or social media links, leadership, and contact information. Make these readily available at any event at your church. Remember, people know it is a church—use this to your advantage by welcoming people and inviting them to come back if they are in the area or if they don't have a church home. Offer a one- or two-minute greeting to all who may be visiting. You may wish to note that you will be at the reception and happy to answer any questions, especially if there are features of the building—or other programming—that may be of general interest. Be creative.

Scott Gunn, executive director of Forward Movement, talked with me about his experiences striving for excellence:

I grew up in the Community of Christ church where everyone is a volunteer, including the pastor, and I started playing the organ and singing in middle and high school. Attending St. Mark's Cathedral in Minneapolis for Evensong, the liturgy wasn't just excellent, but transcendent. It seemed like the heavens had opened, joining our voices with the angels and archangels. It felt like it was a little bit of earth and a little bit of heaven all together. It's not just about musical competence. Having a doctorate in organ performance doesn't equate to transcendent liturgy; it takes heart to understand what is happening and help people feel it also. For me, excellence came to mean the ability to offer the very best in a sacrificial way. Everyone can offer this kind of excellence. I want to be competent and good at what I do but it is not a performance; it is an offering to God's glory. Striving for excellence—no matter what our ministry or church looks like—is something we can all do because it is people pouring out their best for the glory of God. The world needs Jesus, and the need is real, and our church can share Jesus with excellence. This is less complicated than we think and harder than we think. It is difficult but not complicated work. I would love to make a bumper sticker that said: "It's not about you! It's about Jesus."

What are the guides for excellence? Here are three Scott shared with me:

- Pray a lot—remember it's not about you. You don't have to figure everything out on your own, and when you fail it's not the end of the world.
- Humility—we still have things to learn. It gets exhausting to pretend we have all the answers.
- Honesty—speak the truth in love.

Our job as leaders is to look ahead and make sure we are all going in the right direction.

Part of being committed to excellence is in the ways we may plan liturgies that include other languages or cultural references. One of my biggest pet peeves is when people assume they can lead a service in Spanish because Spanish is phonetic and they have read something in Spanish before. If there is no one who reads, speaks, or sings in Spanish and there is a dire need for a service in Spanish, by all means, use that high school Spanish and help. If there is a better, more excellent way to bring Spanish into your service, then please do it.

"But, Sandra, we cannot find any person of color/Latina to represent, to read, to preach, to lead." I have heard this repeatedly. I never know how to keep a loving face when I hear that statement. People often say this to me when I ask about the lack of diversity in people, liturgies, songs, or languages spoken at an event, service, or workshop. That is one reason we need to have respectful relationships with people who are not like us. We must stretch our arms, like Jesus, and have relationships with people who do not look, think, or act like us. That is evangelism. That is important. When we have respectful relationships, we will try to do things more excellently when we are using other languages or other cultures. Even more, because we will have formed respectful relationships, people who are not like us—people from other cultures, younger people, LGBTQI+, and so on—will be at the decision-making table and will voice their opinions.

Because we have these respectful relationships, people will feel encouraged and empowered to speak up when they feel that they are not being represented in a respectful and excellent way. Our job as people of God is to continue inviting others to the table, listening and helping them feel included, welcomed, and valued. Part of the commitment to excellence is listening and respecting people's suggestions.

Another part of being excellent is having excellence in how we share our church with the world. Roger Hutchison, director of Christian formation and parish life at Palmer Memorial Episcopal Church, talks about the importance of church branding. He says that the goal of branding is to convey the message of Jesus's love, lower barriers of entry and participation, and involve the whole church community in the sharing of the good news. When we decide to brand ourselves, we are stating that we are serious. We are committed. As Roger says, that branding must show Jesus's love. Is that branding only focused inward or do we know that we can use it as an evangelism tool? Do we want to settle for the logos we have had for years or will we decide to update our branding to showcase who we are today?

As you consider updating your logos and brand, review your mission and vision statements. Those should lead you where you hope to go. Once you review and update your mission and vision statements, compare to see if your logos, ads, and branding reflect what you believe. Do not make the mistake, however, of thinking that rebranding will bring youth or families to your church to stay. Flashy new things may bring people in the door, but what will keep them is still relationships, excellence, authenticity, and love. Your commitment to share God's love and Jesus's forgiveness in an excellent way will help keep those who walk in the door.

If you realize that your commitment to excellence means rebranding, consider whether you can pay a firm to help you or if you will have the vestry and a few other creative people involved in this effort. While many would argue that it is the lack of funds that stunts us, it is our lack of creativity or vision that keeps us where we are. If we would like a new logo, we can ask if there is anyone in our congregation who designs or is learning design. Do not copy someone else's idea. You can find inspiration in others' work, but if you steal it and put your name on top of it, it is still stealing.

Although it shouldn't be rushed, it shouldn't take years to rebrand. Plan to spend a few months to a year on this work. If you don't take the time to prepare the congregation for this change, you may cause conflict; if you take too long, boredom and loss of interest may be the result.

Let's look at several important points of branding. First, branding must convey the message of Jesus's love. I have seen many churches that have amazing stained glass windows, art, crosses, and other unique physical attributes. That could be a starting point when rebranding. You can use one of the unique features in the logo or brand. Inclusive, progressive churches may want to include a symbol to signify that all people are welcome and celebrated there. I always look for those sometimes subtle but present signs that a church is LGBTQI+ welcoming.

Second, branding must lower barriers of entry and participation. In other words, people should not feel intimidated by the branding and logos. They should be used as welcoming and inviting symbols for the community. Just as fast-food logos are recognized by people around the world as signifying a place to eat, our logos must indicate that people will get amazing food for the soul when they come to our church. Ideally, our branding should include and welcome, assuring those who see it that they are part of something bigger, part of the good news.

Third, branding must involve the whole church community in the sharing of the good news. Part of using logos and brands is to share that we are part of something. I love seeing people wearing the Episcopal shield because I know that we are from the same church. Likewise, seeing people wearing our brand and logo shows that we are together. We are linked as one body and we are there to share the good news to the community—not just those who come inside our walls, but those who may never set foot through our doors.

When the whole church community commits herself to sharing the good news in an excellent way because she is committed to the collective mission and vision of the church, things will change and thrive. People's lives are transformed, community engagement and mission will be achieved, and the church community will grow deeper in faith and actions.

A helpful strategy in the move toward excellence is a questionnaire. Not everyone will like a questionnaire, but if it is as easy and short as possible, people may be able to overlook the annoyance. If you are part of a smaller church, it may not be difficult to visit every member, although larger churches do sometimes conduct a yearly "every member canvass." The goal is to reach as many people as possible from your church community to see how they are doing and where they see room for improvement. Sometimes it is not easy to visit every member, but it may be possible to call every member and have contact in that way.

It has been my experience that people of color may not click "respond" to a questionnaire unless personally invited. *La gente Latina* and other cultures have been brought up not to volunteer unless personally invited. I grew up in the United States, where I learned to volunteer and even toot my own horn (though not easily): two values that U.S. Americans hold dear. We are encouraged to raise our hands and volunteer. We are also encouraged to talk ourselves up. I have seen white males do this effortlessly, but women and people of color and LGBTQI+ and black men may not find it easy. Because we are building respectful relationships, the personal invitation and assurance that another's voice is necessary to the process is work we must do.

In my work with the Episcopal Church Foundation, we create original resources in Spanish. We have leaders in Iglesias Latinas write articles, lead webinars, and share ideas. One thing that continues to impress me is the commitment to produce attractive resources. When we are being excellent and maintaining respectful relationships, we want to show all those who come through our doors or visit our website the same respect. We want everyone to see that all of the languages or cultures represented are valid and celebrated. I was recently at an event located in an area where many *gente Latina* live yet there was not any signage or brochures in Spanish. I was very curious about it because I had never noticed this lack until holding a Spanish-language event there. It is not too difficult or expensive to have things translated and posted but it does take planning, commitment, and vision. Sometimes we do not even realize who is missing from the decision-making table. Is everyone represented and are there accommodations for those who need them?

Activities

Walk around your facilities. Note if they look poor, average, good, or excellent. How can you improve?

Ask an honest friend to visit your church as a "mystery churchgoer." Then, share their findings with your vestry and others involved in the ministries of your church.

Find a song in a different language or a style that you have never done before. If you need to, find a recording or someone who can help you learn it correctly. Continue to learn it until you feel comfortable enough to sing it at church.

Ministry inventory

This can be done with the vestry or with a larger group, if possible, to have more perspectives. This activity could take more than one day together, especially if it has a lot of energy behind it. This activity may be toughest for the people who have been in the church the longest.

Take an inventory of your ministries, programs, weekly events, services. Write down everything you are doing. Make sure to include what you are doing in community engagement as well as within the congregation. Include those things you do periodically (raise funds for a specific purpose by doing a garage sale), and those things you do seasonally (Advent walks, Easter egg hunt).

After you make the inventory, write down who provides the leadership for each program or ministry. Who is involved? How many people does it serve? While you are noting this information, also identify which ministries are for children, youth, young adults, families, and so on. Identify which are for the target group you are most trying to reach. Identify how much money is being spent on each of the ministries. Identify which ministries are bringing in money. Have people with whom your church has connected in community engagement ministries come to the church? Have they been invited to come and be a part of the church? Has anyone become a member because of one of these ministries?

Prayerfully look at your ministries and put them through your strategy filter. Are all of these programs and ministries helping your church live into your mission, vision, and call? Finally, as a team, decide which ministries and programs will stay, which will be discontinued, and which will be modified or updated. Keep copious notes on why you made specific decisions for each program or ministry. This step is the toughest, but it must not be skipped.

Capítulo 3: Excelencia

Hay algunas personas que se sienten mal ante la palabra "excelencia" porque la comparan con la perfección, y hay algunas que prosperan cuando se les presenta un desafío para mejorar. Leemos en Filipenses 4:8 "Por último, hermanos, consideren bien todo lo verdadero, todo lo respetable, todo lo justo, todo lo puro, todo lo amable, todo lo digno de admiración, en fin, todo lo que sea excelente o merezca elogio". Esto nos anima a mantener la excelencia en mente. La gente crece, y también deben crecer nuestros programas, música, folletos y bienvenida.

Para algunos, la palabra "perfección", al igual que "excelencia", conlleva recuerdos negativos, perjudiciales o incluso injustos. Para mí, la excelencia es pasarme horas aprendiendo una nueva canción. No me gusta no estar preparada. Como no puedo leer música a primera vista, debo hacer mi tarea antes de cualquier evento en el que voy a cantar. Estar comprometidos con la excelencia puede ayudarnos a estar preparados para lo inesperado. Mi hijo, Ellis, ve la excelencia de esta manera:

> El primer día que fui a visitar la Iglesia Episcopal Grace en Houston, sentí que estaba presenciando un evento comunitario, que era algo que no había experimentado tan fuertemente en una iglesia en mucho tiempo. Los lectores, acólitos, músicos, congregantes y sacerdotes se daban energía unos a otros, y esa energía fue algo que sentí. Recuerdo sentir que los lectores me estaban dando un mensaje importante solo para mí. Levantaban la cabeza y nos miraban mientras transmitían lo que Dios tenía que decirnos ese día. La música se tocó bastante bien, y la variedad fue muy inspiradora. En ese momento, conocía muy poco sobre la congregación, pero presenciar la música me ayudó a comprender la complicada historia de la congregación. En un canto, pude escuchar el cristianismo carismático de diferentes músicos. Podía escuchar las tres congregaciones diferentes que se habían unido con el tiempo para convertirse en Grace. Podía escuchar los diferentes colores, idiomas, y razas de las personas. Pude escuchar a las generaciones antiguas y nuevas pasando su tradición y haciendo crecer una cultura juntos.

Cuando visito iglesias, siempre noto la estética. Veo si las personas están tratando de mostrar lo mejor para cualquiera que entre al santuario. Entiendo que todos tenemos diferentes ideas de lo que se ve mejor, pero las cosas básicas como la limpieza, la organización y la creación de un espacio acogedor son de suma importancia. ¿Qué está tratando de transmitir una comunidad eclesial a quienes asisten por primera vez?

¿Tienes una rampa para las personas que la necesitan? ¿Tienes pasamanos, si tienes escalones, para que la gente se sostenga, especialmente cuando llueve o nieva? ¿Tiene baños que sean seguros y accesibles para todas las personas? ¿Se entrega la comunión a las personas que no pueden caminar hasta el altar? ¿Tiene un equipo que lleva la comunión a las personas que no pueden salir de sus hogares? Todo esto tiene que ver con la movilidad y la accesibilidad y esto se ha vuelto especialmente importante para mí desde que mi papi sufrió un derrame. Debo admitir que, aunque la movilidad y la accesibilidad han sido importantes para mí durante años, lo ha sido aún más porque tengo un ser amado que lo necesita. ¿Qué mejor recordatorio de que las relaciones con personas de todos los ámbitos de la vida es muy importante?

Cuando trabajamos hacia la excelencia, una variedad de personas debe participar en el servicio durante la liturgia. Por ejemplo, cuando visito iglesias, miro quién lee, quién está en el altar, quién saluda, etc. Si deseamos atraer a más jóvenes, debemos tener jóvenes como parte del liderazgo visible. Cuando incluimos a los jóvenes en las reuniones de planificación, podrán decirnos lo que necesitan. Si deseamos atraer a más jóvenes, ¿ofrecemos clases de formación o grupos pequeños para sus edades con líderes capacitados y con experiencia? Las mejores personas para educarte en lo que necesitas para atraer a la juventud es la juventud.

¿Cómo podemos ser excelentes mientras participamos en las actividades habituales de la iglesia? ¿Cómo puede nuestra excelencia ayudar realmente a otras personas a ver el amor de Dios y la invitación de Jesús de venir a él? La excelencia es bíblica—haz todo como si fuera para Dios. Eso ciertamente no significa hacer todo de manera mediocre, sino que significa hacer todo lo mejor que podemos.

Planificar con mucha anticipación también brinda la oportunidad de organizar eventos que se centran en constituir una comunidad y llegar a aquellas personas que no son parte de la iglesia. Al igual que con cualquier otro evento, se puede invitar a la comunidad por adelantado a través de volantes o las redes sociales.

Tenemos que prepararnos de antemano cuando vamos a tener eventos a los que hemos invitado a personas del vecindario. Cuando yo me estoy preparando, lo hago con mucho amor. Quiero que la gente sepa que estoy comprometida con ellos y que son importantes—ya sea un grupo de dos personas o de mil. Estoy comprometida a la excelencia debido a mi compromiso de ser como Jesús, mostrando respeto y amor por las personas.

La preparación y planificación son muy importante. Por ejemplo, es bueno tener una lista rotativa de personas que leerán en un domingo determinado. Siempre planifica y prepárate. En esto se basa la excelencia.

Tengan hermosas tarjetas para las visitas o pequeños folletos que enumeren el horario de los servicios, enlaces a sitios web o redes sociales, nombres del liderazgo e información de contacto. Recuerden, la gente sabe que es una iglesia; usen esto para su ventaja dando la bienvenida a las personas e invitándolas a regresar si están en el área o si no tienen una iglesia. Sean creativos.

En mi trabajo con la Fundación de la Iglesia Episcopal, creamos recursos originales en español. Tenemos líderes en iglesias latinas que escriben artículos, dirigen seminarios web y comparten ideas. Una cosa que me sigue impresionando es el compromiso de producir recursos atractivos. Cuando mostramos excelencia aun en un folleto les estamos diciendo a las personas: eres importante y queremos darte lo mejor. Cuando somos excelentes y mantenemos relaciones respetuosas, queremos mostrarles a todas las personas que entran por nuestras puertas o visitan nuestro sitio web el mismo respeto.

CHAPTER 4

Authenticity

But there's one thing we know
Even when we are confused
Faith and love lend a hand
United we face the truth
We are strong, we survive
And we hold on as we cry
We are strong, we survived.

"We Are Strong" / "Somos fuerza"
—text and tune by Sandra Montes

This is one of my favorite subjects—and one that gets me in a lot of trouble as I ask questions like:

- Why isn't there much diversity in your slate of conference leaders and presenters?
- Why does the group picture of this important event—for example, young adult ministry, women's retreat, preaching event—only include white people?
- Why was the first person of color I was able to see in your church or diocesan staff page a sexton, treasurer, IT specialist, or nursery worker?
- Why wasn't someone from that culture playing that African drum?
- Why did a monolingual white person read the gospel in Spanish during a diocesan or church-wide service?

The list can go on and on, but I will stop here, for now.

I have been pondering these questions for the past thirty years as a Latina in the Episcopal Church and, sometimes, things don't seem to be getting better. I am certain they have, yet we still have a long way to go to truly be a beloved community and inclusive or affirming. It feels at times that we take one step forward and two steps back. That may be a great way to dance to a Spanish song, but it isn't the best way to be authentic in our church.

For us as individuals and as a church to be truly authentic, we must authentically represent the breadth of our membership—and our neighborhoods—in decision-making leadership positions. For example, if I am hosting a youth event, those leading the event and making the decisions must be youth. If there is to be a cultural event, people from that culture must be the ones putting it together and making the decisions about it. So, if the event is called "Jamaican Festival," the people leading it must be Jamaican. Similarly, if there is a position called Missioner for Latinx Ministries or such, the person in that position must be Latinx.

If you are planning a Mothers' Day Out program, mothers should be planning it and leading it and asking other mothers what their needs are. Otherwise, we are not being authentic and not helping others get what they need. I know some of us think we understand what it's like to have a young child because we have grown children, but life has changed drastically since we were mothers of young children. So, the people making decisions must be mothers with kids of the same or similar age as those we are trying to reach. Does that mean that I, as a mother of a young adult, shouldn't be involved? No. It means that I, as a mother who will not benefit from the program, will defer to a mother who could benefit from the program. Not because my wisdom, advice, knowledge, and experience do not help, but because we want to lift up the voices of those the program is designed to support.

If we are not part of the group the program is benefiting, we must remain in the margins and invite other voices to the forefront. For example, when I have been invited to lead music for a youth event, I always prefer to lead the team of youth and facilitate the discussions, but the decision-making and actual event leadership is done by the youth. Not because I cannot do it, but because when people see themselves in places of leadership, it encourages all of us, reminding us that we, too, could be in leadership and are welcome. That is the ultimate purpose of this authentic sharing of leadership: to be like Jesus, who included and empowered everyone.

The question often arises: How do we get more people of color in our church, seminary, program, diocese, and so on? My answer is by including us in decision-making bodies, by giving us the seats of privilege at the table, by making us something other than an afterthought, by asking us what we need and want, by seeing and listening to us. The only way to have people of color, LGBTQI+, people who are differently abled, and others representing the full range of humankind in leadership is by being authentic. It can be difficult for those who do not consider themselves part of a "minority" community to be invested in the work of inclusion.

As we think about inviting people from other cultures, people who speak different languages and represent other races and countries, into our Episcopal (and maybe mostly white) spaces, we must be authentic and respectful. I imagine this is not easy if you have never spent time with people of other cultures. Traveling to places where you can still speak English—in a country whose language is not English—is not truly being exposed to other cultures or languages. That is just being on a privileged vacation, even if it's called a mission trip.

Spending generous amounts of time with people who seem unlike you is important for ministry. And, all over the United

States, where our mainline churches are "dying" or dwindling in numbers, our reality is that if we go outside our doors, as we are commanded to do, we will find ourselves in the midst of people of all sorts of backgrounds, languages, colors, abilities, beliefs, and they are all looking for an authentic connection. If we have never been around people who appear unlike us, how are we going to enter into respectful relationships with our neighbors? How are we going to prepare excellent resources or spaces for them without their input? How can we be authentically transparent and vulnerable, recognizing that to enter our doors may feel like potentially entering an unsafe and scary space?

We mistake reality, as in reality television, with authenticity. Jesus is an authentic leader and showed us how to lead authentically. Jesus knows who he is. Jesus is not concerned about being popular. He is an authentic leader who teaches by the examples we find in the Bible and in the lives of others. Authenticity can be felt and is captivating. Jesus's authentic love calls us to him. What are we doing in our ministries to be authentic so others will want to come to Jesus and learn more about him? What can we do to be authentic and not part of a "reality" life? Jesus says, "For I have set you an example, that you also should do as I have done to you" (John 13:15). Jesus showed us how to relate to others when he washed his disciples' feet. He taught us what to do when he advocated for that "sinful" woman and dared others to throw the first stone. He taught us what to do when he touched the untouchables and healed on the Sabbath. Who are the untouchables, the sinful, the unclean of today? Trans people, homeless asylum seekers, interracial children, fat people, people in wheelchairs? Who? Sadly, we all have someone in mind and for many of us it is ourselves.

Can you imagine what it looked like for this man, a clean, well-known, charismatic person, to actually touch and speak with an "unclean," untouchable person? I can imagine it because that is exactly what has happened in my life. I have often felt unclean and sinful and untouchable, but Jesus is often seen with me, is not ashamed of me, loves me. Jesus would take selfies with me and come to my birthday party because that is the God we follow. Everyone else turned their faces away and abandoned people who were "unclean" but Jesus didn't. Jesus shared the good news with them, and often cured them.

How can we be this Jesus to those around us? When we encounter others, and we show our authentic Jesus-centered selves, we can help them come to that same authentic knowledge of Jesus's unconditional love.

Authenticity can take many forms. For example, how are you working to provide liturgical and other print resources for those whose first language is not English? If a free internet translation site, rather than finding a well-qualified translator, is the only way you are providing materials in other languages, perhaps you are not being authentic and authentically Jesus-centered.

When asked to be the one person of color to give an opinion or a suggestion, I've often been told, "We will share your opinions with the rest of the planning team." The rest of the planning team is usually all white, monolingual, mostly male, and high church. I have finally found the strength and voice to say, "No, if you want my opinion, you must have me or someone who is like me at the table." It is very difficult for a lot of us classified as "the other" to be open and speak up. Sometimes we feel that we finally made it to the decision-making table and we don't want to lose that spot, so we may stay quiet. Authenticity is not only the seat at the table but the safe space in which to speak our Jesus-centered truth.

Side note: Some of us who have been called "token" many times are afraid of saying no when we are invited to participate in an event, be part of a panel, lead a workshop, be part of a planning team, and so on because we are certain nobody else who is like us will be invited to take our place. This doesn't happen because we are so unique or so talented—even though we are—but because people usually tell us they could not find another person of color, another trans person, another person with a disability, and, "We tried!" We often feel guilty when we can't participate, and that is a huge responsibility.

This is why it is so important for those of us in leadership to ask those who are not sharing or those whose voice is in the minority if they would like to speak. Inviting someone to speak or share an opinion may not elicit a response, but it is a start. If the person is the only person of color, or the only LGBTQI+ person, or the only person with a disability in the room, it may take several invitations for them to feel safe to share. It is up to the leadership to make sure everyone's voice is being heard for there to be authenticity.

Being authentic requires respectful relationships and excellence. To use a song or a prayer from a different culture or language, first understand what it says, why it is important, and how to pronounce the words correctly. The best place to go for this information, when striving to be authentic, is to a native speaker or someone from that art form's culture.

Sometimes, churches will include a prayer, song, or altar cloths from other cultures and there is no reason for doing it except they were curious or it looked cute or it was *Cinco de mayo*. The first question is always: Why? Why do you want to include a song in a language nobody in your congregation speaks? Why do you want to use a *sarape* instead of your regular altar cloths? Why do you want to make an altar for the *Virgen de Guadalupe*? If your answer is I don't know; I think it's cute; I think it's what we are supposed to do, then please stop.

When we want to add something to our aesthetic, like a *sarape* or a *Virgen de Guadalupe*, we must understand the meaning of these items. There are sacred items that have specific uses. If you don't know what an item is, where it comes from, or how to use it, then the best option is not to use it. If you still want to use it, then you must find a way to understand it. A commitment to authenticity means you will have a reason for including something new, different, outside the norm. Does this mean never using, singing, wearing, or speaking anything that is not part of your own culture? No. It does mean that there will be a purpose for incorporating it that is authentically centered on Jesus.

Part of being authentic is knowing who we are as a congregation. Sometimes, churches invite me because they want to have a Spanish service or want to start using Spanish songs in their music program. Although Spanish speakers are all over the United States, there are some neighborhoods where we are not present. I have been invited to lead a workshop on authenticity and diversity or to sing only Spanish songs in some churches where there isn't a Spanish-speaking or Latino presence or where the church has not done the preliminary work of relationship building, and it is extremely uncomfortable for the congregation and for me. For those churches to be authentic, they must see what their congregation truly needs. If I am invited to help the church devise a plan to go into the neighborhood to invite *la gente Latina* who live around the church, that is being authentic.

What holidays are we celebrating? You'll recall that part of doing things excellently is to plan ahead. What holidays are you including in your plans? Are you including any that are not representative of your congregation or even of your surrounding community? If it is something that belongs in your community, are you asking your community to help and be part of the planning? Are you celebrating *Día de Muertos*, but don't have any people from Mexico or other countries and cultures that celebrate the day? Are you being authentic or buying decorations from Party City? Remember that we must always have respectful relationships, and when we do, we will not celebrate holidays that we know nothing about. It is not respectful or excellent or authentic for me to celebrate a beautiful holiday that has deep meaning that I don't understand. When I am in the homes of friends who have altars and celebrate *Día de Muertos*, I love participating and asking questions at an appropriate time. It is beautiful and meaningful and touching.

I have seen many churches embracing *Día de Muertos* in the most beautiful, respectful, and authentic ways. That is one way of bringing in the community, especially if it is a community that has not been involved in your church yet is part of your neighborhood. Some churches bring in experts to give classes during formation time to help churchgoers understand the celebration of a tradition or special holiday and how to do it respectfully and authentically. Formation is key when committed to the work of authenticity. Some churches invite musical groups and make the celebration into a community-wide event. This is appropriate and creates an opportunity for the church to open her doors and reach people who may have never entered the property. People will be grateful that you are celebrating a beautiful holiday such as *Día de Muertos* in an authentic way.

Regular feedback and one-on-one sessions are important so everyone—volunteers and committee members, lay staff, congregation, and pastors—is on the same page and everyone knows the expectations for practicing the faith authentic to your congregation. Reiterate the vision and mission of your organization every time you meet; hopefully these include excellence and authenticity. I remember one of my favorite supervisors, Miguel Escobar, would summarize the expectations of my job every single time we met for our monthly one-on-one conversations. This helped me to stay focused and to understand what my role was. I was often doing things that may not have been part of my original job description, but the basics were the same. If you have respectful relationships with everyone involved and they are all striving for excellence and are committed to authenticity—which evolves with the congregation—they should not be surprised when you ask them to grow.

While it can seem very different to hold these conversations about authenticity with volunteers rather than paid staff, there are excellent ways to speak with our volunteers about our commitment to excellence and authenticity. Eric Law has some wonderful suggestions for church volunteers in his *Holy Currencies* book. There must be feedback meetings with volunteers to keep everyone current. As people who are committed to Jesus, all volunteers and paid staff must have constant training and reminders of who we serve and why we serve. When we are all conscious that this work is for the up-building of the larger community, we are free to be authentic in our love of Jesus, self, and neighbor.

I once worked in a parish that hoped to reach those in its neighborhood with a regularly scheduled "mariachi mass." While I love mariachi music, it is the music of a specific Latina community and not *la gente Latina* as a whole. The liturgy was more appealing to the Anglo congregation than to those in the neighborhood. The mariachi group also found it difficult to listen to feedback and was not willing to learn new, more liturgically appropriate songs. Because of the historical relationship with the group—one without a respectful, authentic, shared commitment to excellence—the congregation's leadership felt very awkward about speaking honestly with the mariachi group. Yes, as the next chapter talks about, we must be loving because all of this is of God. And, we must also be loving to our community and our future community. As we decide to be authentic, we must also decide what can remain and what needs to be tweaked and what must completely change or go. The foundations of respectful relationships, a call to excellence, and the hard work of discovering our authentic way of following Jesus are essential to the difficult conversations that will always accompany this work.

For us, with the mariachi, we left it unchanged for a few weeks and realized it wasn't working. They were not being excellent and we definitely were not being authentic for our community. We decided to invite them to be with us once a month, and they were asked not to wear their mariachi outfits because the music was not going to be all mariachi music. I tried to rehearse with them, but they were not used to learning new music. Then, we made the decision to let them go, with the possibility to ask them to return for special events. In other words, our new-found respectful relationship allowed us to speak in a way that we all felt heard and understood. Our commitment to excellence would not let us remain in contract with them and our resolve for authenticity in worship and music also contributed to the dissolution of the contract. Was everyone happy? No. Were there people who were vocal about their disapproval? Yes. Was everyone OK—eventually—and was the ministry better for choosing authenticity and excellence? Yes.

As an activist and evangelist, I often post about authenticity on social media and speak about it in front of groups. I have often given this example when I want to speak boldly about disrespectful practices.

I usually get at least a couple of people who come to me or message me to say something like: "Does that mean I can't ever sing a song in Spanish or play a maraca because I'm white?" People can become defensive when told—or challenged—that what they have been doing for a long time is disrespectful. Oftentimes, people—including people of the culture they are mocking—have never asked them to stop.

A note about those of us who smile or even encourage you to continue singing, dancing, appropriating our culture. *La gente Latina* have been taught, from birth, to be polite, as have many people of color including Native Americans and Asians. We are happy and grateful you want to learn from our culture.

We usually believe you mean well. But, that doesn't mean that you should continue doing it. Once we know better, we must do better.

One particularly painful but necessary conversation for any discussion of authenticity concerns mission trips. My parents have painful memories of missionaries: memories of them making more money than those working within the local economy, having the best houses and things, including food, and not sharing it with those they were there to serve. Those missionaries often did not establish respectful relationships with the local people and did not do things with excellence, nor were they authentic. They felt they knew best what the people needed, and expected people to be grateful and not complain.

There are thousands of pictures online of well-meaning white people taking pictures (usually selfies) with poor or dirty dark children. I have heard this called the "white hero" or "white savior" mentality. The thing is, as Christians, we believe that the only savior people need is Jesus. And, a white Westerner may be able to share the good news with others in very different contexts, but is that authenticity?

I have seen groups of Christians going into other countries to help build schools or churches. That is amazing. The thing is, what happens when they leave? Have they (the missionaries) left the congregation, community, or town the tools they need to continue with the ministry in that space? Have they left the community with resources to help them help themselves? Have they done the homework beforehand to know what the community needs and what the earth in that locale can provide? Have they built the respectful relationships ahead of time to know what to bring to the community? Have they been excellent in their actions to know what will help people and not hinder them?

Mission work, for it to make a difference, needs to be a partnership with those we are trying to help. We are, after all, sharing

Jesus. We are reminding them of the good news that they are loved. How will they see Jesus if all we are, as ambassadors of Jesus, is a candy machine or a cute accessory provider? There is nothing wrong with taking candies, and clothing, and so on. But, is that all it is? Is there nothing we can do that will go deeper in faith and be Jesus to them?

Authenticity means doing everything genuinely, not trying to feed our ego but trying to feed others' souls in a most valid, trustworthy, faithful way. Something that truly changes us more than them. I wish cameras were banned from mission trips. I wish nobody could have "proof" that they were helping others, except that when people came back, others would be able to see that something had changed, something was different, something was transformed.

When those who represent every aspect of our church's spiritual journey have been invited to the decision-making table, we will be able to celebrate all, not just what we presume to be appropriate and appreciated. This is ministry *with* the full community and not ministry to or for "others." I have often been the token Latina at events. I cannot stress this enough: when you are inviting people who are new to the table, you must make it feel safe for us to communicate. I am always grateful when a leader says, "Sandra, you have not said anything yet and I would really love to hear your opinion on this issue." I feel visible and empowered. When we are committed to authenticity, we will want every voice to be heard and we will create the space and sense of welcome for the voices to speak.

I have been asked several times: "What do we do if we don't have any diversity in our congregation or community? There are only white people all around us!" This may be true in some places, but not most. However, there are other kinds of diversity and other ways to reach people who may not live near you. There are most likely a range of people who work in those mostly white communities. They may not live in those neighborhoods or own property there but they are working there. So, how can we authentically serve them?

You guessed it, begin with respectful relationships. You must get to know them. How do we do this? By going where they are. Are they cleaning houses in the neighborhood? Are they cleaning your parishioners' homes? That is a perfect way to start a relationship. Are they your baristas or restaurant helpers? No matter where they are, you can start having a relationship with them. Once you establish a respectful relationship, you can talk about church stuff. Or, if you are a pastor who wears a collar, you can wear your collar every time you go into a shop or restaurant. They will recognize that you are a religious person. You may then start having even more relationships by offering "free coffee with prayer" or asking if they would like you to bring communion or ashes or Advent wreaths. There are many ways to start relationships with authenticity.

There are many churches that offer Alcoholic Anonymous or other similar meetings. These often begin because the pastor or a parishioner felt the need to start one in the area. Remember that even when another group is sharing your space, you can still foster relationships, excellence, and authenticity by sharing who you are and that you are available to them beyond their time in their meetings. Remember that people who come to your church know it is a church. They know that there are pastors and that there are service times. An attractive brochure and signage can provide visitors with information. Have your chapel or sanctuary open with someone available for prayer or spiritual conversation.

I encourage churches to have adequate signage with service times, attractive brochures that spell out a range of programs and services available, and clearly marked sacred space open for prayer whenever there is a garage sale, fundraiser, car wash, or any other activity being held. People are always looking for a connection and it is great when we can provide a spiritual one for them.

Being authentic takes courage and commitment. Authenticity helps us let go of our ego and accept others as they learn to accept us. Being authentic is understanding what our gifts are and living into them. This is both personal and congregational. For example, a worship director understands what the strengths of his worship band or choir are and encourages growth and excellence in the members. This does not mean that they do not go out of their comfort zone at times, but it does mean that they do the best with what they have. They do not try to imitate or be someone else. They continuously improve their style of worship—which should be informed by the congregation— and musicality.

Authenticity also promotes trust. When we are authentic, we know who we are, we know what we want, we know where we are going, and we know what we need to know to get there. When we are inauthentic, we project phoniness and this does not lead to trust, but rather makes others feel uncertain around us. Often when we are inauthentic it is because we are lost. A congregation must journey inside *first* to get clear on her values, strengths, passion, and vision. When we are not grounded in authenticity, we will behave in inconsistent ways that can cause others to lose trust in us, and therefore we will not be able to help them get to Jesus.

One first step on our quest of being authentic and finding our purpose is to answer, as individuals, and then as a congregation, the following questions, in no particular order.

- What is vital to you?
- What motivates you?
- What are your strengths?
- What is your ultimate goal?

These questions have the possibility of changing your life toward your full potential as authentically you. When answering these questions, honesty and introspection are most important. Try to forget what others expect of you and your congregation. The answers to the questions will change with your age and experience. What was most important to you when you were eighteen is probably not the same as what is most important to you now at forty-five or seventy-five. Similarly, what our church's strengths were in 1989 may not be what her strengths are today. Answer these questions with the first thing that comes to your mind. Of course, you can "fix" whatever you need to later. See the activities section for suggestions on how to do this individually and with your congregation. This authenticity activity goes hand in hand with excellence.

I asked my friend Miguel Escobar to share what he feels is authenticity in the Episcopal Church, and he said:

> I believe that authenticity and its opposite—inauthenticity— is closely connected to honesty and lies. As a gay man who grew up in a small, conservative town in Texas, I am very familiar with lying for the sake of survival. As necessary as those lies may be for a time, there is a profound cost because the closet means choosing over and over again to live inauthentically, trapped in a cage of lies. Joining the Episcopal Church was a part of my process of leaving the closet behind so as to live with greater integrity. It is hard to emphasize how important this is for spiritual wholeness. In John's Gospel, the Holy Spirit is described as a Spirit of Truth, and I've found that living in this Spirit requires me to be authentically rooted in who God made me to be. At a fundamental level, we'd lose a lot of authenticity were the Church to return to requiring LGBTQ people to remain in the closet to serve in ministry.

Authenticity is being rooted to something. It means being original, honest, and truthful with our self. When we are authentic, we welcome others and give others permission to be authentic also. This may not be easy for a lot of people. You may have been taught to be polite, to not make anyone uncomfortable, and to avoid confrontation, as I was. When doing the work of the gospel, we sometimes are faced with uncomfortable topics, changes that are difficult, and times of passionate dialogue. The important thing to remember is that we are siblings in Jesus, and as such, we must act like Jesus. (Which, you'll remember, also includes making a whip, driving out people from the temple, and overturning tables.)

Sometimes we want to believe that Jesus only had one mode: peaceful. Although Jesus spoke about peace, justice, and love, he never said that in order to achieve peace one must never speak up or feel passionate about things. He shows us that he is passionate about God's house and God's word. He is passionate about us and those in the margins. He is passionate about the people who are discarded or outcast. He is authentic and passionate about authenticity. "Throw the first stone," he dares us. Be truly honest with yourself, he is saying.

The thing is, we must see who we have respectful relationships with. When I am speaking to groups about authenticity, I ask them to look at their last ten to fifty pictures on their phone (depending on how many they take) and see who is in them and who is missing. This usually will give us a glimpse into what we find important. This will also show us with whom we spend our time. Is everyone white? Does everyone look like us? Is there diversity of any kind?

After asking people to look at their camera gallery, I ask them to check their social media. Who are their friends? Do they have friends from all walks of life and ages? Do they have friends in other countries? In other states? Do their friends speak other languages? What do they post or share? Do their posts highlight other cultures or other languages? Do they share stories about diversity and justice? How can we be authentic in our diversity in music, dress, food if we are not diverse in our friendships, social media posts, or pictures?

Authenticity, vulnerability, and transparency go hand in hand. This is why it is difficult to be told you're being perceived as not being authentic. It takes vulnerability and humility to admit that we are being egocentric and acting as though we know best, even if we don't. There is a fine line between celebration, appropriation, and ignorance.

When you are in relationship with people from another culture and want to learn from their experiences, it is likely that you will not want to appropriate their culture, but rather celebrate or appreciate it. Cultural intelligence, or CQ, can be an important aspect of our growth in authenticity. Having cultural intelligence means that a person has the capacity to function effectively in a multicultural environment. In our terms, multicultural includes people who have different abilities, different sexual orientations, different colors of skin, different languages, and so on. In the Episcopal Church, that definitely includes people of color. Church leadership must employ CQ as a way to foster tolerance, enhance cross-cultural interactions, and reach others.

What does that mean? When we are exposed to other cultures, we are more likely to have tolerance for others. For our ministries, tolerance is not enough. However, that may be where we start. Authenticity and diversity do not happen quickly. It takes time, commitment, patience, exposure, and love. When I use the word "other," I often use quotation marks because it is a widely used term that can encapsulate how the dominant culture sees the rest of the world. It is a divisive and classist view of the world.

There are many ways to increase our cultural intelligence and to bring more understanding and breadth to authenticity, especially in ministries. First, we must be aware of who we are and how we see others. When we are being honest with ourselves, we will see the ways we classify and divide ourselves from others. Most of the time when I walk into an English-speaking Episcopal church in the United States, I am very aware of my color. I look around the room to see if there are other people of color and if there is room for me. When other people of color are present, I can relax, as though I am among family. Since my dad's stroke, I am also more aware of people with limited mobility and the spaces that are not designed with them in mind. Consider the ways in which a space—and those who share that space with you—make you feel: When do you relax and breathe more deeply and when do you feel yourself "on edge"? What can you learn from those physical and emotional responses about yourself and the unconscious ways in which you may classify others?

We must have humility, especially when we are in ministry with others. Adopt the position of a student to learn about other people and cultures—let them teach us and share with us what is important about their culture, practices, beliefs. Different does not mean wrong, though we may have been taught to see differences through that binary lens. Books, sermons, small group sessions can lead to invitations for people from other cultures to share their food or music with us. Those invitations may become reciprocal, as we visit places of worship that seem completely foreign to us. The more authentic experiences we have with other cultures, the more we can be changed.

One thing that I am still learning to do to increase my cultural intelligence is not to hang out with the same people all the time. When I attend an event in my diocese or in the wider church, I usually find people who are like me—women, women of color, people who speak other languages, and so on. I have been trying to expand my reach and my circle because I know that will help me be more authentic in my life, ministry, and work. Oftentimes, we seek the comfort of being around people who think like us, look like us, vote like us, have a similar educational background as us, or the same marital status as us, because it is predictable and safe. But, if we are working to be authentic, we must extend ourselves and go beyond what makes us feel safe. There are many people who need Jesus and his love and we, when we can extend outward, can show them that authentic love.

As we continue our respectful relationships with others, we can show hospitality and authentic radical welcome. During this time, we have to listen instead of speaking. It is exciting for some of us to get to know others and we may have been taught that we cannot allow a lull in the conversation. But being hospitable to another does not mean it won't be uncomfortable. Allow for the pauses, the silence in the act of authentic listening. The gift may be to have another's perspective as we learn together and talk about Jesus, the Bible, and our beliefs.

Another option for our REAL work is accountability. When we are committed to authenticity, we may need some partners who are honest and will hold us to our promise and commitments. When we choose to be authentic and want to grow our cultural intelligence, having a partner in that work is encouraging and will keep us on track. As we make goals for our commitment, we can share with another person about reaching our goals or when we are not able to meet them. It is always nicer to walk with people, holding each other accountable, especially when we are choosing a life that is more like Jesus.

For this work of authenticity to be fruitful, we must ask God to show us, through the reading of the Bible, through spiritual formation with others, and through prayer, our biases and walls that must come down. This ongoing commitment requires time and energy. When we are devoted to authentic and life-changing formation that draws us closer to Jesus, it will be a daily choice to allocate time for reading, praying, and sharing with those who join in the commitment to authenticity.

Activities

I Spy

Just like we appropriate clothing and other items of fashion, congregations can appropriate traditions from other cultures. Look around your building at your art, your aesthetic. Look at your liturgy, music, prayers. Is there something that belongs to another culture or tradition that you have adopted without truly knowing why? As a group, consider why.

The "whys" have it

In pairs, answer the following questions:

- What is a tradition you hold dear? Why?
- What is a tradition you hold dear at church? Why?
- What are you holding on to at home that you feel you can't let go? Why can't you let it go?
- What do you think people would be angry about if it was taken out of your church? Why?
- What activities do you think are no longer authentic for your congregation? Why do you think you're still doing them?
- What is a tradition that you know is not really authentic to your faith community? *Cinco de mayo*? *Día de Muertos*? (*Cinco de mayo* is, literally translated, the fifth of May. Some people think it is Mexico's independence day because it sounds similar to the Fourth of July. It is the celebration of the Battle of Puebla when the Mexican troops beat the French invaders. *Día de Muertos*, or Day of the Dead, is not a Mexican version of Halloween. Though related, the two annual events differ greatly in traditions and tone. Sure, the theme is death, but the point is to demonstrate love and respect for deceased family members.) Why are you doing it? How could you make it authentic?

Who are you? Who is your congregation?

Ask these four questions to get to the core of who you are as an individual and as a church. The honest answers will help you see who you are authentically and help you live into it.

What is vital to you?

Individually: As you think about what is most important to you, put aside all the things you think you should or should not care about. Make a list of what you know is important to you; these are your core values. Once you have written down the values you have, note the top five. Then, ask yourself if you are reflecting your authentic self in your values. Do your values dictate how you live, behave, make choices, and communicate?

With the congregation: Make a list of what the congregation thinks is important and ask yourselves as a group if the church's values reflect how you are living as a community. Look at your church budget. Do your values direct where you're spending money? For example, if as a church you say that you are hoping to attract or serve more youth and you have not allocated money for the youth program, your ideal value and your authentic value are not in sync.

Go deeper personally: We may answer family or faith or education instantly when asked what is most important to us because we have been programmed to think of those things as our core values. But, if we are honest and look at our spending habits we will see what is truly important to us. Check your bank account for the last couple of months. Where are you spending your money? We spend our money on what we feel is necessary or what is important to us. Our bank accounts will show if we love getting coffee or a magazine, if we are spending on what we say is important or on things we could live without. Our spending habits will show us if our hoped values are in line with our authentic values.

What are your strengths?

Individually: This is a tough one for a lot of people. What do we do well, innately? We can all learn to do many things but there are some things that come naturally to us—some of us call these our God-given gifts and talents. Many people focus on their weaknesses and don't see their full potential. List your strengths or take a quiz to help you. Be honest about your strengths. You can make a three-column list of what you are innately good at, what you have learned to be good at, and what you wish you were good at. Once you have honestly named your strengths and talents, you can see if what you are doing professionally and in ministry is in line with your core values and with your strengths in order to live most authentically.

With the congregation: Enumerate the church's strengths and gifts. What does the church do well? Are you great with liturgy? Is your music excellent without much effort? Are you good at throwing big events? You will notice that the talents and gifts of the people in the congregation also drive what the church is good at. When we don't know our strengths, we miss out on opportunities to share them with our congregation. It is important to take inventory of what your strengths are so that your church can do authentically great things for the community and the kingdom.

What motivates you?

Individually: What helps you get out of bed in the morning? What do you love passionately, what sparks excitement in you when you think about it? What gives you life? Jot down the first thought you have without thinking if it is "right" or "wrong." Does your passion align with your core values and with your strengths and talents? Are you working professionally in a field that is related to your passion? Is your ministry work related to your passion?

With the congregation: Ask this question and ask participants to yell out their answers related to ministry or faith. Jot them down. Does your mission statement reflect what your congregation feels passionately about? Are you living into your mission authentically and passionately?

What is your ultimate goal?

Individually: What do you want? Where do you hope to end up? What is your vision for your life? If you don't have a vision statement, how could you write one?

With the congregation: Revisit your vision and mission statements. Do they reflect where your church is going? Do they reflect what your church is called to be and do?

Technology

Make a Pinterest board of authentic and inauthentic pictures around culture, socioeconomic status, sexual identity, racism, religion. Share and find a good time to discuss.

Using social media, invite people from your congregation to share pictures or videos that show their culture and diversity.

Capítulo 4: Ser legítimo

Este es uno de mis temas favoritos y que me mete en muchos problemas.

He estado reflexionando sobre el racismo, la falta de diversidad, y la falta de respeto hacia la gente que es marginada en este país y nuestra iglesia durante los últimos treinta años como latina en la Iglesia Episcopal y, a veces, parece que nada mejora. Estoy segura de que ha mejorado; sin embargo, todavía tenemos mucho por recorrer para ser verdaderamente una comunidad amorosa e inclusiva o afirmativa. A veces parece que damos un paso adelante y dos atrás. Esa puede ser una excelente manera de bailar una cumbia, pero no es la mejor manera de ser legítimos en nuestra iglesia.

Para que seamos verdaderamente personas legítimas o auténticas, debemos representar auténticamente la amplitud de nuestra membresía—y nuestros vecindarios—en posiciones de liderazgo y en la toma de decisiones. Por ejemplo, si estoy organizando un evento juvenil, los que dirigen el evento y toman las decisiones deben ser jóvenes. Si va a haber un evento cultural, las personas de esa cultura deben ser las que lo organicen y tomen las decisiones al respecto. Entonces, si el evento se llama "Festival de Jamaica", las personas que lo dirigen deben ser jamaicanos. Del mismo modo, si hay un puesto llamado Misionero para Ministerios Latinos o algo similar, la persona en ese puesto debe ser una persona Latina.

Ese es el propósito de este auténtico intercambio de liderazgo: ser como Jesús, que incluyó y capacitó a toda la gente.

La única forma de tener personas de diferentes culturas, LGBTQI+, personas con capacidades diferentes y otras personas que representan a toda la gama de la humanidad en el liderazgo es ser auténticos. Puede ser difícil para aquellos que no se consideran parte de una comunidad "minoritaria" invertir en el trabajo de inclusión. Y, eso pasa en muchas de nuestras iglesias donde sólo hay personas blancas. Aun cuando nos aceptan o invitan a ser parte del ministerio, no nos dan voz ni voto.

Por eso es muy importante para el ministerio y para la iglesia pasar mucho tiempo con personas que parecen diferentes a nosotros.

Jesús es un líder auténtico y nos mostró cómo liderar auténticamente. Jesús sabe quién es él. A Jesús no le preocupa ser popular. Es un líder legítimo que enseña con los ejemplos que encontramos en la Biblia y en la vida de los demás. La autenticidad se puede sentir y es cautivadora. El amor auténtico de Jesús nos llama a él. ¿Qué estamos haciendo en nuestros ministerios para ser auténticos para que otros quieran venir a Jesús y aprender más sobre él? ¿Qué podemos hacer para ser verdaderamente auténticos? Jesús dice: " Yo les he dado un ejemplo, para que ustedes hagan lo mismo que yo les he hecho" (Juan 13:15). Jesús nos mostró cómo relacionarnos con los demás cuando lavó los pies de sus discípulos. Nos enseñó qué hacer cuando abogó por esa mujer "pecadora" y desafió a los otros a tirar la primera piedra. Nos enseñó qué hacer cuando tocaba a los intocables. ¿Quiénes son los intocables, los pecadores, los inmundos de hoy? ¿Mujeres trans, solicitantes de asilo, las personas sin hogar, niños interraciales, personas gordas, personas en sillas de ruedas? ¿Quien? Lamentablemente, todos podemos pensar en una persona "intocable" o "inmunda" y para muchos de nosotros somos nosotros mismos.

¿Te imaginas cómo se veía este hombre, una persona limpia, conocida y carismática, tocando y hablando con una persona intocable e "inmunda"? Me lo imagino porque eso es exactamente lo que ha sucedido en mi vida. A menudo me he sentido inmunda, pecaminosa e intocable, pero a menudo se le ve a Jesús conmigo, no se avergüenza de mí, me ama. Jesús se tomaría fotos (*selfies*) conmigo y vendría a mi fiesta de cumpleaños porque así es el Dios que seguimos. Todos los demás volvieron la cara y abandonaron a las personas que eran "inmundas", pero Jesús no. Jesús les daba buenas noticias y con frecuencia las curaba.

La autenticidad significa hacer todo genuinamente; no tratar de alimentar nuestro ego, sino tratar de alimentar las almas de los demás de la manera más válida, confiable y fiel. Algo que realmente nos cambia más que a ellos. Desearía que se prohibieran las cámaras durante los viajes misioneros. Desearía que nadie pudiera tener "pruebas" de que estaban ayudando a otras personas, excepto que la gente pudiera ver que algo había cambiado, algo estaba diferente, algo se había transformado.

Hay muchas iglesias que ofrecen reuniones para Alcohólicos Anónimos y otras reuniones similares. Esto a menudo comienza porque el pastor, la pastora o un feligrés sintió la necesidad de comenzar uno en el área. Recuerda que incluso cuando otro grupo comparte su espacio, puedes fomentar las relaciones, la excelencia y la autenticidad al compartir quiénes son y que están disponibles para ellos. Recuerda que las personas que vienen a tu iglesia saben que es una iglesia. Saben que hay pastores y que hay horarios de los servicios. Un folleto atractivo puede proporcionar información a las visitas. Mantén tu capilla o santuario abierto con alguien disponible para la oración o acompañamiento espiritual.

Ser una persona legítima requiere valor y compromiso. La autenticidad nos ayuda a abandonar nuestro ego y aceptar a los demás. Ser auténtico es comprender cuáles son nuestros dones y vivir dentro de ellos. Esto es tanto personal como congregacional. Cuando una persona es legítima, no intenta imitar o ser otra persona. Siempre está mejorando y tratando de ser la mejor versión de sí misma.

La autenticidad también promueve la confianza. Cuando somos auténticos, sabemos quiénes somos, sabemos lo que queremos, sabemos a dónde vamos y sabemos lo que necesitamos saber para llegar allí. Cuando no somos auténticos, proyectamos falsedad y esto no conduce a la confianza, sino que hace que otros se sientan inseguros a nuestro alrededor. A menudo, cuando no somos auténticos es porque estamos perdidos. Una congregación debe conocerse primero para aclarar sus valores, fortalezas, pasión y visión. Cuando no nos basamos en la autenticidad, nos comportaremos de maneras inconsistentes que pueden causar que otros pierdan la confianza en nosotros y, por lo tanto, no podremos ayudarlos a llegar a Jesús.

Le pedí a mi amigo Miguel Escobar que compartiera lo que él siente que es la autenticidad en la Iglesia Episcopal, y dijo:

> Creo que la autenticidad y su opuesto, la falta de autenticidad, están estrechamente relacionadas con la honestidad y

la mentira. Como un hombre gay que creció en un pueblo pequeño y conservador en Texas, sé que he tenido que mentir para mi supervivencia. Por muy necesarias que sean esas mentiras por un tiempo, hay un costo profundo porque no ser yo mismo significa elegir una y otra vez vivir sin autenticidad, atrapado en una jaula de mentiras. Unirme a la Iglesia Episcopal fue parte de mi proceso de dejar atrás el clóset para vivir con mayor integridad. Es difícil enfatizar cuán importante es esto para la integridad espiritual. En el Evangelio de Juan, el Espíritu Santo se describe como un Espíritu de verdad y he descubierto que vivir en este Espíritu requiere que esté auténticamente arraigado en quién Dios me hizo. En un nivel fundamental, perderíamos mucha autenticidad si la Iglesia volviera a exigir a las personas LGBTQ que permanecieran en el clóset para servir en el ministerio.

Para que este trabajo de autenticidad sea fructífero, debemos pedirle a Dios que nos muestre, a través de la lectura de la Biblia, a través de la formación espiritual con otros, y a través de la oración, nuestros prejuicios y muros que deben derrumbarse. Este compromiso continuo requiere tiempo y energía. Cuando nos dediquemos a una formación auténtica y transformadora que nos acerque a Jesús, será una elección diaria fijar tiempo para leer, orar y compartir con quienes comparten el compromiso con la autenticidad.

CHAPTER 5

Love

Remain in me like I remain in you
Love one another as I have loved you
With my life, with my soul
I have given all of me because of love

"Remain in Me" / "Permanece en Mí"
— text and tune by Sandra Montes

ove plays a central role in diverse, multicultural, and multilingual ministry. Although in my acronym, REAL, love is the last word, love is all throughout being real and being a follower of Jesus. Love is the last letter of REAL to signify that it is what holds the rest together. It is the foundation, the root, the most important of all. When we have love, everything else will be doable; when we have love, everything is possible. When we have love, we will be able to form respectful relationships, we will strive for excellence in all we do, and we will be committed to authenticity.

As Christians our ultimate commandment is to love God above all, to love ourselves, and to love our neighbors. How do we love God? With all our mind, body, strength, soul. How do we love our neighbors? As we love ourselves. How do we love ourselves? As though we are God's favorite child. Because we are. This work is a labor of love. Love is not just the best way, it's the only way. Jesus taught us about love and says: do likewise.

When we are trying to include those beyond the people who attend our church regularly, we must do it in love. When we love, we want the best for the people: we want them to feel relaxed, welcome, included, and loved. Love propels us to be the people we are called to be. I want to be the best version of myself because I love. Jesus has called each of us by name.

When we reach out in love to those beyond our walls, we are more likely to put ourselves in their shoes. We will remember what it was like not to be included. We will remember what it was like to long for love and welcome. We will remember what it takes to be visible and to be accepted. We will remember what it was to be on the outside looking in.

When we love, we are committed to our church, our community, and the world. We are committed and want the best for our commitments. When we are committed to sharing the good news with everyone around us because we love God and neighbor, we will work to forget our fear or continue forward in spite of the fear. We will seek to help people encounter Jesus every single time we are together. When we love, we are committed to listening to others. When we listen, we are able to understand what people need. We are not trying to give people what we think they need, but through love we are able to help them genuinely.

As people who love, we can commit to pray for every person who passes through our doors and for anyone who is touched by our ministries. Prayer is one of the most powerful disciplines we Christians have and when we pair it with love, it can move mountains. People who don't believe in miracles don't notice the miracle of love. Miracles manifest themselves in various ways to different people. What all miracles have in common is that they come from God's incredible love.

When people who have been invited into community through respectful relationships have decided to stay because they have seen our church's commitment to excellence and feel welcome because of our authenticity, they will continue to grow in faith because of our love. They will know us because of our love. They will notice that, although we are not perfect, we are committed to our love of God, self, and neighbor.

As Christians, if we just have respectful relationships, we are doing what a lot of people hope to do. There is nothing wrong with being in respectful relationships and many churches stay there. There are churches who help their neighbors with food and clothing and never invite them to come to church, never pray over them or tell them the good news that Jesus loves them unconditionally. It is always great to help, yet we are called to do more.

There are churches who do things with excellence and invite the community to partake in that. People around the community are invited to well-prepared concerts around Easter and Christmas. Churches have beautiful services and special events with well-known musical guests, preachers, and actors. Some churches participate in community events and share their wealth by hosting galas and silent auctions for special causes. And, many do not take these opportunities to share Jesus's love with those who attend through a word of encouragement or prayer. People leave these excellent and extravagant events smiling, but with not much else.

There are churches who are authentic and make sure that all of their diverse, multicultural, multigenerational, and multilingual events are done with respect and high quality. These churches have done their homework and open their doors for others to lead. Some churches open their doors to everyone and think this is enough, and don't provide more information or conversation on Jesus and the good love news.

When we do all these things, these wonderful, necessary things, but do not include love, we are being good neighbors. This is important work and we are called to do this also. But above that we are called to love. If we don't have love, as 1 Corinthians 13:1 tells us, we are a noisy gong or a clanging cymbal. Love is what takes us from being a social club, an outreach program, a social justice entity into deep life-changing, life-giving, life-altering territory. It is when we include love and God that we take what others are doing and give people the good news. As churches, our expression of love looks a bit different than that of secular organizations. It looks, sounds, and feels like God and Jesus and the Holy Spirit moving all throughout our activities.

As Christians, we believe that God transforms us. We believe in Jesus giving us life through his death. We believe that the Holy Spirit guides us and that all three, in one, are with us everywhere we go. As Christians we have a love that can transform others—and that love is what this world needs.

There is a huge need in our world—people are longing and dying for love. People are lonely, people are suffering, people are in pain. There are people all around our churches who are looking for that love that doesn't require them to earn it. There are people all around our churches watching us to see if we are truly bringing Jesus and Jesus's love to the world. When we open our hearts and give people love, we are going into a deeper relationship. We are getting into family territory. As children of God, as followers of Jesus, as believers, we have life, we have love, we have hope, we have a future.

Love is what keeps us going. Love is what we long for. Love is what most of us are looking for in a community and especially in a church.

When all else fails, love doesn't. When I started working for the Episcopal Church Foundation as the Spanish language resources consultant, one of the first things I wanted to do was ask people what they thought Episcopal identity was. "What does it mean to be an Episcopalian?" I asked person after person, including the newly elected Presiding Bishop Curry. I did not know what I was going to hear.

As a person who came from the evangelical tradition, I wondered if people were going to have many different perspectives.

I thought that people who came from the Roman Catholic tradition were going to talk about the differences between both churches; that they would note that priests could marry, or that women could be priests. Or, that there was no difference because, in the United States, our Spanish-speaking congregations are often made up of those who brought with them Roman Catholic traditions—first communions, veneration of the Virgin (especially the Guadalupana in some parts of the country), and *Posadas*. I, honestly, was wondering if people even understood what being an Episcopalian meant.

Time after time, I heard things like: "I was invited to be a reader for the first time!" "I was invited to have a leadership role even though I was not married to the father of my children!" "I was included and accepted even though I am a single parent!" "I was asked to cook something for a potluck the church had." "My children were included in the Christmas pageant even though it was our first time to go to church." Story after story of acceptance, inclusion, and of course, love.

I was smiling from ear to ear hearing all these amazing stories. I understood what they were saying: such gratefulness and joy when we spoke about our churches and our denomination. I kept thinking, "That is why I am glad I am in the Episcopal Church and why I don't leave even on the worst day."

Nobody mentioned the liturgy. Nobody mentioned the music. Nobody mentioned the sermon. Nobody mentioned anything except the inclusivity, acceptance, and love. I realized over and over again that my expectations for this exercise were so low. I expected people to talk about what happens inside an Episcopal church that keeps bringing them back. But they all spoke about the true way, the true reason for church. They spoke about the good news that we all receive when we come to meet Jesus. And, it's not that they did not find it in another church, but rather it was about something more, about an expansion of what they had learned in other places. Love was what put it all together.

Many of us come from traditions with many rules to follow. If we didn't follow all the rules, we weren't allowed to have any kind of leadership or even community. For example, I could not lead music in several churches because I am a woman. Also, when I was invited to sing at evangelical or nondenominational churches after I found the Episcopal Church, often I had to omit that I was divorced and that I was an Episcopalian. It is refreshing to be in a denomination that has space for women in leadership and for people with pasts.

We have great news to offer the world. When we are meeting people around our neighborhoods it is important to remember that many of them are seeking something. Many of them have been beaten up by the Church and need us to be gentle and patient. They may be looking for love and Jesus. If we start with love, we cannot fail.

That is why love is so important. As we are establishing respectful relationships, offering excellent options in worship, community engagement, and resources, and as we are bringing our authentic selves, wrap everything in love. When we remember that love is the way, the only way, and when we assure others that they are loved, God's love can change people's lives. We can all tell a story about someone's love that transformed us. Some of us have had amazing faith leaders who have shaped us by showing us unconditional love. Others have had incredible examples of love in our homes. Our parents or siblings have been agents of love and inclusion and they have helped us to want to give that love away to others who need it.

When we are loving, we are also growing. When we are growing, there will be growing pains. This is when the true test begins. When we are not comfortable, we will see how we are as a community. For example, when an English-speaking congregation welcomes Spanish speakers into their churches, there can be great joy and excitement because the relationship is new. The community welcomes the new siblings, may have some shared meals, and starts the path to partnership. As the Spanish-speaking cohort grows, so may discomfort. Do we rethink service times? How might we share space so that both language groups can worship in ways that (at least initially) feel authentic? Sometimes we may realize that to show love is to give the "other" group the prime time spot. Many non-English services that are housed in monolingual English-speaking churches are held after noon. Sometimes, they are as late as 5 p.m. How do we navigate this?

This time difference sometimes hinders respectful relationships because the people who come to the "early" service will not stay for the "late" service to have some Coffee Hour relationship-building time. Same goes for the people who attend the "late" service. There can be some overlapping times and churches could use this as a great way to bring all people together. This takes planning, commitment, a lot of effort, and even more love. It is not always easy to bring people together. If respectful relationships are an authentic goal, then a combined Coffee Hour may become the place where people go to feel like they are part of a larger community.

When we have established respectful relationships, we can have the tough conversations in love. There is usually not an easy answer to issues like service times or stewardship campaigns, or bilingual services during an important holy day. Be prepared that people can have passionate opinions and may say some painful things to others. When we have a culture of love, these holy, messy, and uncomfortable conversations can happen, should happen, and we can have honest conversations, not arguments, about the hot topics.

Love covers a multitude of sins, the Bible says. Because it covers a lot of sins, it covers many other things—discomfort, confrontation, arguments, disagreements, and mistakes. When we are working through respectful relationships, excellence, and authenticity, it will take love to become a family. The important thing about being family is that we can share, disagree, agree, and everyone continues to belong to the family, even when it gets heated or difficult.

Make no mistake, there will be times when we will mess up. We may say the wrong things, we may do the wrong things, we may use the wrong pronouns, we may even misgender or call someone by a wrong name. In our effort to become acquainted and share our lives, we may find that we have been appropriating a culture, or saying some words incorrectly. We will mess up. And that is why love is most important. That is why we must always cover ourselves and others in love. Love will allow us to apologize and forgive. Love will help us face our shortcomings and uplift others' successes.

Latinxs are one of the fastest-growing groups in the United States, but it will take much love to keep us within the Episcopal Church, helping the church to be strong and grow in numbers and spirit. What does that love look like? The kind of love *la gente Latina* and Asians (the other fastest-growing group in the nation) seek is the kind of love that requires hours of companionship and relationship building. The kind of love needed to thrive within multicultural or multilingual groups is the kind of love that learns to say please, thank you, excuse me, and welcome in other languages—not by using apps but by having conversations with people from other countries and learning to be a minority in some spaces.

A great way to show love is to learn how to pronounce and spell someone's name. There is nothing wrong with grabbing a pen and paper or your phone to jot down the name of someone you have just met, asking them to spell and pronounce it. There is nothing wrong with asking people to repeat their name, as you repeat yours, or to remind you how their name is pronounced. It shows respect, excellence, and authenticity when you are committed to learning someone's name and, if it is too difficult to learn quickly, to write it down and have it with you. This goes hand in hand with knowing people's pronouns also.

There are people who will not speak up and correct your pronunciation or spelling; be aware of that potential (culturally based) difficulty. Part of the respectful relationship work is to get to know someone's culture and customs. When you have respectful relationships, you will understand little by little what their cultural norms are and how you can be respectful and authentic, even as you are learning people's names.

Another way to show love for people who speak other languages or are different in a variety of other ways (sexual orientation, abilities, looks, and so on) is to ask them how they would like for you to share about their experiences with racism, ableism, homophobia, or traditionalism. For example, your new friends are not going to be everywhere you are and, although you want to be respectful of their story, you may be in a situation where you can share their story to help others. (It is important to have their permission when sharing, even if it seems harmless or insignificant.)

Being uncomfortable together is part of being in a loving relationship. It is also part of a loving congregation and their worship. There is no way to please everyone in your congregation, especially if you have a diverse group with different needs and preferences. If there is no way to please everyone then some will be uncomfortable at any given time in a service. It could be during the beautiful classical anthem that people may appreciate but not enjoy. It could be during the sermon when the pastor speaks about difficult and controversial current events. It could be during communion when some children run to the altar rambunctiously. There are plenty of times in the service when one can feel uncomfortable. When we are doing all of this with love, we will be ready for these times and will have a balance in the liturgy, music, prayers, and customs of the congregation.

Being loving also means that your congregations' needs, important events, and interests are your priority. Does this mean only the pastor and vestry have a responsibility for being present in congregants' lives? Certainly not. Formation is always a key element to any of these four values. This is especially important with newcomers. The parish and its leadership must show up to births, hospital stays, deaths, and other life-altering situations and celebrations. Being present at congregants' important life events is often seen to be the pastor's role but, for loving churches, it is a shared role. Yes, the pastor is important and people, whether we agree or not, still see them as representative of the church. As we continue to form people we can dispel those presumptions.

I have been very fortunate to be able to spend time with people from a wide variety of congregations. It is always a treat to hear about the way different congregations do things. It is great to see how people grow, how people fail and get back up again, and hear the stories of love and joy. I feel especially blessed to have spent time with very diverse congregations who continue to have hope because of their love of God and each other. They continue to believe there is a future and that they have a purpose. Often, within their midst are people who have come from other denominations who want to give love back because of how they have been loved in the Episcopal Church, even when there have been challenges.

It is not easy to be a welcoming and loving church, especially when we are not used to having to adjust our lives for others. When we are used to doing things a certain way and have thought that way works, it is very difficult to change, unless you include love. Remembering to translate all materials or going to the expense of hiring an interpreter is difficult.

Remembering to ask about pronouns or pronunciation can be difficult. When we are including other voices around the table, we must do it with love, thinking about those others, beloved of God, and their needs. Loving people is Jesus's commandment: not a suggestion but a commandment.

"I stayed because people showed me love." I remember speaking with a lay leader about how she got to her church. She said she had been invited by someone who attended the church (respectful relationship). She said when she attended she felt very welcome because people greeted her warmly and she loved the music and the sermon (excellence). She said she also felt very welcomed by the Spanish language service that included music and other elements that she held dear as a person from Latin America (authenticity). She said, however, that if she had not felt loved she would not have stayed. She told me about the other churches she had visited. They had similar values to this one, but there was something missing. She felt she was always a visitor and never part of the family. However, in this church she had felt like they took her in and loved on her. When we are thinking of giving up, remember, when we have love, we have it all.

Our response to God's unconditional and ever-flowing love is sharing that love with others. Who loved you so much that you continued to attend that service or that organization or that dinner group? Love is so important but, ironically, we often forget it in our churches because we are so busy with logistics or liturgies or anthems or potlucks or community engagement or budgets. Do everything in love. Sometimes we can quote it but we can't do it.

Try to remember the time when you realized you were loved by God. How did you feel? How did you find out that God loved you? Did someone tell you? Did you hear it in a sermon? Did you read it in the Bible or another book? Did someone's life reflect God's love so clearly that you believed it? Did you hear it in a song? Did you feel it during an illness or a tragedy? Did you hear it as a child but didn't believe it until you were an adult? Have you realized it?

I often ask couples to share with me their love story. I especially love asking people who have been together many years. It is sweet to see how the retelling sparks something in them, and in anyone listening. Love is a miracle though not easy to maintain: it takes energy, commitment, time, strength, and courage, among many other things. Love is not impossible, but definitely not easy.

Similarly, love in Church can be difficult to maintain and to nurture. It is a daily commitment to say yes. You can't just say yes to Jesus once and be done. It is a lifelong commitment that may even lead to the question, "Why am I still here?"

That is how life in church is. Jesus calls us, the Church, his bride, a tough image for some of us. But, if we are to be his bride, then we are committing ourselves to Jesus, his teachings, and his commandments, even when that comes with daily questions and doubts.

When we add love to commitment, and when we are committed to love, that 1 Corinthians 13 kind of love, we will be able to face the challenges. Love has a way of giving life where there was only death, as at Lazarus's resurrection. Love has a way of healing when there is only illness, like the woman who had been suffering from hemorrhages for twelve years. Love has a way of setting people free when there is only bondage, like the man from the country of the Gerasenes. Love has a way of giving us hopes and goals and dreams where there was only defeat and setbacks.

This is what we have to give others. This is what lives inside us as Jesus followers. This is the hope we can give the world, especially those close to us. There are people who need to hear about this love and have never heard of anything like this. There are people who seem our opposites who need love and want to hear about love and are ready for you to share love with them.

I was brought up in the evangelical tradition. I was born into it and actually liked to go to church. I loved singing the hymns, I loved listening to my dad preach and my parents sing, I loved playing with my brother and other church friends (when my dad wasn't giving me *the look* from the pulpit). Some pastors in our previous denomination said that Roman Catholics were going to hell. They talked against the Virgin Mary. I grew up knowing that we could not have images of the Virgin or the saints or Jesus. We had empty crosses, if we had any. We believed in the Bible, as written (or so we said). So, when I came into the Episcopal Church and saw a huge crucifix, an altar, a rail, my dad wearing a dress, and the kneelers, I looked at my mom and said, "We are going to hell!"

As the years went on and I realized that God had given us such a gift and blessing by leading us into the Episcopal Church, I wondered what would have happened had we not found it. I have that better-than-thou attitude about some (extreme conservative) people and about some (extreme conservative) beliefs. I roll my eyes (mostly in secret) at what some people believe or hold on to. For the longest time I didn't understand people's seeming obsession with holy water, blessings, not taking communion, and so on. Little by little, with a lot of respectful conversations, with a lot of experiences, and with a lot of love, I am learning to be more patient with myself and others.

Part of being loving with people who do not think or look like us involves patience and flexibility. I have seen my dad so open and willing to do what people need, even if others raise their eyebrows at it. For example, many people have come to my dad for holy water. We come from a tradition where that seems more like a magical potion than something religious or spiritual, but my dad blesses the water and they take it with them to bless their home or their family members.

When we encounter people who have traditions that we do not understand or who want us, as leaders, to include a song or prayer or practice, we must listen in love. When we establish respectful relationships in love, we are telling people that we are interested, we want to honor them, and we want to be in community with them. Before they understand what we do at church, we must understand what their experiences have been and what they need. Does this mean we have to change all of our liturgy and music to accommodate one new person? No, but we can think of a way to incorporate what people need and would appreciate for their own spiritual growth and nurture.

One pastor who also grew up in a more evangelical or traditional church told me a story about being loving to his new congregation. He moved to the United States after a divorce and took a church in one of the most Mexican areas of the city. When he arrived, he observed and started fostering respectful relationships. He noticed that most of the people who went to his church were from Mexico. He also realized that life as an Episcopalian in the United States was very different from being an Episcopalian in Latin America. He continued to form relationships with the people in his church and started getting to know their lives and their needs.

He also noticed that several saints adorned different parts of the church building but one was missing, *la Virgen de Guadalupe*. He noticed that people talked about their devotion to her, but nobody mentioned why they didn't have an altar for her in the church. Although he did not venerate her, he knew she was very important for the community, not only inside the walls but also the community around their church.

Because he was committed to excellence and authenticity, he invited a few friends who venerated *la Virgen, la Guadalupana, La Lupita, La Morenita* to talk about her, the history, and the faith surrounding her. He was told story after story of how people connected to her, about her miracles, and about how people felt so close to her, as a mother figure. They told him about the community activities surrounding her and that they had seen the parishioners attending, but never a clergy person. That is when he asked his secretary and the vestry why their church, centrally located in Little Mexico, had never participated in the *Virgen de Guadalupe* festivities.

He was told that the pastor who was there before him had a strict rule that there was not to be any veneration or altar to *La Guadalupana*. Two pastors before, an altar had been installed and the previous pastor had taken it down. It had split the large group that used to attend. Although they still had a good average Sunday attendance, many had left. Little by little he put together all the pieces and as they were approaching the *Guadalupana's* day, he asked the vestry to put together a program in honor of *La Virgen de Guadalupe*.

There was renewed energy and excitement surrounding this event. People from the neighborhood were invited to several small meetings and events leading up to the day, December 12. Because he had been studying and talking so much about her, he felt a rekindled love for Mary and also started understanding his parishioners' dedication and love for Our Lady of Guadalupe. He was careful to do things authentically and continued to have a few people for counsel and direction, taking a step back to allow the lay community leaders to lead the way.

When the day finally arrived, there was so much energy and hope and the community came together. He says he did not ever imagine having so many people participating in a caravan around the neighborhood, not only venerating Our Lady but also praying for the community. Tears of joy rolled down many people's cheeks as they saw people who had left their church come back to take part in the historic event. He said to me, "I could have said no, because that was not my tradition and I did not understand it. But I decided to be a loving pastor to my flock and I am glad I did." Now, the tradition continues and year after year more faithful come to the event. Had he not been committed to love, how different things might have been.

Love is the most important thing for any of God's work to be done. We are commanded to love and to be known by our love. We are called by name to love others who are also called by name. Sometimes we forget that the same God that loves us and calls us and wants the best for us is also rooting and loving and blessing the person we may not like very much. As Christians we believe there is one God and that God created us all, all of us. Everyone in the world is our sibling. The people we have problems with are also created by God and loved deeply by God. Our siblings are in other faiths, traditions, countries, and cultures.

Love, the Bible says, bears all things, believes all things, hopes all things, endures all things, and never ends. That is the good news people are longing to hear and experience. Love hopes all things. I have been asked why I stay in the Episcopal Church when I can seem to be so angry with her. I say, "I stay because I love her and I believe she can do better and I am hopeful for her." Love hopes all things. I may not always believe all things, but with the love only God can give me, I can. I don't always bear all things, but through the love God gives me, I can.

Love never ends. That's the kind of love the world needs. The kind of love that doesn't end even when we want to give up. The kind of love that doesn't end even when we don't agree. The kind of love that doesn't end even when we are so far from each other. The kind of love that doesn't end even when I've done something really bad. That is the love that God has. Oh, God, help me have that same love for my siblings who still may have not experienced that kind of love.

Love is what will keep us coming back to church. Love is what keeps us believing there is still work to be done even when our church attendance has dwindled. Love is what will send us out into the world to love and serve God in our neighborhoods and beyond. Love is what will help us seek out others to start having respectful relationships. Love helps us be committed to excellence and seek to be authentic in all we do.

Wendy Pineda was looking for a place to have her *quinceañera* a month before she was turning fifteen. This is very unusual because people spend months, if not years, planning the elaborate and traditional celebration. She knew she needed a church to have the Mass, one of the important parts of the *quinceañera*. She looked around for a Roman Catholic church because that is where her parents went once or twice a year. She had been baptized and had celebrated her first communion in a Roman Catholic church near her house but did not remember the last time she had attended Mass.

Her mom worked for a school at that time and a friend from work heard that she was looking for a place to have Wendy's *quince*. She told her about the church she attended, San Mateo, which was very close by. She told Wendy's mom that she was sure that San Mateo would have her *quince* and that there were not many requirements. The church Wendy had gone to before required at least two years of attendance before they would have the *quince*.

The first time Wendy went to San Mateo it was October 31; there was a concert. Cindy Castellanos was playing the saxophone and also did a rap. Wendy had never heard or seen music like that at church. She often felt bored at other churches. She did not know church could be fun. She was blown away and always remembers that experience as the first time she encountered God.

She remembers that, even though she enjoyed her first experience at San Mateo, she was going to give the church only three weeks—the same amount of time it would take for her to turn fifteen. My dad, the priest, told Wendy's mom that he would be happy to do her *quince* and that she would have to attend church and youth group for six months—this could be done before and after the *quinceañera*. Wendy started going to youth group, where she realized some of the youth were from her high school. Even though Wendy felt welcome and included, she always took her best friend, Lucía Guerrero, with her as her "security blanket," promising to do her algebra homework.

Wendy began developing a great respectful relationship with Alex, my brother, who had begun the youth group. She would get to church early to have conversations with Alex before youth group started. She never felt judged by Alex or like she had to know everything to be a leader.

Because her family was not prepared to have the *quinceañera*, they decided to postpone it and have a "sweet sixteen" celebration instead. She remembers that she knew she could leave church and come back six months before her birthday to prepare, but something clicked during those three weeks that she had given to San Mateo. She said that she tried downplaying that she enjoyed going to church. She would tell others that she was just following the rules for her upcoming celebration and that is why she stayed.

Throughout the years, Wendy began inviting close friends to church with her. She says it is difficult to get unchurched people to go to church, and she would usually say, "I'll go out with you on Saturday and let's do my thing on Sunday." One specific time she remembers bringing one of her friends, Natasha Rodriguez, to the English service at San Mateo. Because her friend was not a churchgoer, she did not know what to expect. Everyone at church was dressed up, but Natasha came in jeans and Converse shoes. She felt so uncomfortable. To make matters worse, her three-year-old son started running around and at one point ran up to the altar. The preacher picked the young boy up and continued without missing a beat. At the end of the service, Anne Grizzle, who had been preaching, approached Natasha to thank her for coming to church and especially for bringing her child. Natasha began to cry. Wendy says this memory is one of her favorites because Natasha created lifelong relationships with others because of that very positive first encounter with church. "Looking back, you can look at all the moments you felt God's love and it only takes a second to share that love. Take every opportunity to share it."

Wendy, because of those examples, is very conscious about striving for excellence in all she does, especially in ministry. She says that we need to be excellent within our self, with our friends, our congregation, and then the wider church. "You never know who's looking at you and you never know how people come to God or the church. We all have off days but if you really are who you say you are, people around you will notice."

Wendy, at thirty-four years old, is still accustomed to being the "young token Latina." She says that at the beginning, it was funny to be the only person of color and the youngest at events, in leadership, or on planning teams, but it has since become sad and disappointing. When she can't attend an event, "I feel like I have to carry the weight of providing people with the names of people they can invite to take my place. That is not fair, but I hope that the people who come after me do not have to feel that same burden."

Her suggestion is that we should all surround ourselves with people who are different from us because if we don't have a diverse group of friends, we are missing out tremendously. If we are trying to reach out to other people, we must immerse ourselves in that community to know what we're missing, and we have to do it from the heart because we can all tell when someone is being fake or is trying to use us. "You have to talk and listen to my needs and wants instead of telling me what I need. That's important in all relationships. You have to build a relationship to know when a person is afraid to speak up." Sadly, we are taught to see our differences instead of what we have in common.

What has kept Wendy in the Episcopal Church are the deep authentic relationships built on love. "That right love that fills a void can carry you a long way when it's exactly at the right moment," she says. The example of the loving relationship she had with Alex has helped her mirror that with her godchildren. "That respectful loving relationship with Alex has shown me how to treat a younger person. I never felt stupid; I never felt like a dumb kid. I can't pinpoint that moment when our relationship shifted to becoming lifelong friends, but that is what I want with my godchildren."

Love has helped carry Wendy throughout the time when her mom got sick a few years back. "When I think back at dark moments, I think of who was the shining light. In dark moments different people showed me what God's love was because I needed to see it. While I know that God's always there and is always taking care of me, I needed to be reminded." And this includes the love of the people she met at San Mateo almost two decades ago who have carried her through some very tough times when she did not know what to do.

One reason Wendy will not leave the Episcopal Church, even with its challenges, is that she feels like there is still a place for her. She is not the same person she was when she entered the Episcopal Church at fourteen. She has changed, she has grown, her tastes have changed, and she can still find a community that accepts her and loves her for who she is in that moment. "And in five years, when I have changed some more, I will also find a community; it may not always be the same church and same community, but there's always a place where I fit."

Wendy is now a Kanuga board member. She has played many roles in the Episcopal Church at large and locally. She has been involved in youth, young adult, music, and Latino/Hispanic ministries since she started going to San Mateo. She has been part of the planning teams for the young adult festivals at General Convention, *Nuevo Amanecer*, and Hispanic Missioners Gathering.

She has also given workshops and webinars on money management and stewardship. Wendy prefers to be behind the scenes and learn the history behind the work being done. Professionally, she is a successful CPA and accounting team manager in Houston, Texas. She continues to use her gifts, experience, and knowledge in the church and beyond. Wendy is a great example of what respectful relationships, excellence, authenticity, and love produce.

Activities

Answer the following questions in pairs:

- What are we doing out of love?
- Who are we reaching because we love?
- What, in our mission and vision, points us to love?
- Have you come to this church or stayed because of love? Share a story about this.

Love your neighbor as yourself

What are the things you do to treat yourself when you need a pick-me-up (a spa date, a movie, a date night, a massage, dessert, a book, a mani/pedi)? Make a list of these things. Now, pick a person from the community you are getting to know and gift them one of these.

Self-love

If you could speak with your twelve-year-old self, what would you say? How would you encourage yourself at that age or any other age that was difficult for you? Choose a picture (if you have one) of that difficult age, hold it in front of you, and encourage yourself. Remember these words as you continue your journey.

"Speed dating" or "How to get to know each other quickly"

This game is better for partners, but if you have an odd number, you can divide into triads instead. The most important thing is for everyone to get a turn. Have several questions ready for people to ask each other—they can choose which question to ask and answer. Each person will have thirty seconds to answer the question. Have someone with a loud alarm or use a drum or cymbal to call time. After the two people answer one or more questions, switch partners.

Possible questions:

- How do you show love to someone in your family?
- How did you meet your significant other?
- Do you have children? Tell me about them.
- Do you have a pet? Tell me about it.
- What took you to church for the first time?
- What do you like most about your church?
- How long is your commute to church?

After the game, ask people to share their answers or their thoughts with the group.

Social media love

Post something you love about your church on social media this week. You could share a picture with one of your church friends, a picture of your favorite stained glass window, a video of the reading or the sermon, a sermon quote, or something similar. Try to have a church hashtag so others can find the church posts easily.

Capítulo 5: Amor

En inglés la siguiente letra en REAL es A de autenticidad, pero en español, sigue la A de amor.

El amor es de suma importancia en el ministerio diverso, multicultural y multilingüe. Aunque en mi acrónimo, REAL, el amor es la penúltima palabra, el amor es el fundamento para ser real y ser un seguidor de Jesús. El amor es lo que mantiene unido el resto de los valores. Es la base, la raíz, lo más importante. Cuando tenemos amor, todo lo demás será posible. Cuando tenemos amor, podremos formar relaciones respetuosas, nos esforzaremos por la excelencia en todo lo que hacemos y nos comprometeremos a ser legítimos.

Como cristianos, nuestro mandamiento más importante es amar a Dios sobre todo, amarnos a nosotros mismos y amar a nuestro prójimo. ¿Cómo amamos a Dios? Con toda nuestra mente, cuerpo, fuerza, alma. ¿Cómo amamos a nuestros prójimos? Como nos amamos a nosotros mismos. ¿Cómo nos amamos a nosotros mismos? Como si fuéramos los hijos favoritos de Dios. Porque sí lo somos. Este trabajo es un trabajo de amor. Jesús nos enseñó sobre el amor y dice: haz lo mismo.

Cuando amamos, queremos lo mejor para las personas: queremos que se sientan relajadas, bienvenidas, incluidas y amadas. El amor nos impulsa a ser las personas que somos llamadas a ser. Quiero ser la mejor versión de mí misma porque amo. Jesús nos ha llamado a cada uno de nosotros por nuestro nombre.

Como personas que aman, podemos comprometernos a orar por cada persona que conocemos. La oración es una de las disciplinas más poderosas que tenemos los cristianos y cuando la combinamos con amor, puede mover montañas. Las personas que no creen en los milagros no notan el milagro del amor. Los milagros se manifiestan de diversas maneras a diferentes personas. Lo que todos los milagros tienen en común es que provienen del increíble amor de Dios.

Hay una gran necesidad en nuestro mundo—las personas anhelan y mueren por ser amadas. La gente está sola, la gente sufre. Hay personas en todas nuestras iglesias que buscan ese amor que no les exige que lo merezcan. Hay personas alrededor de nuestras iglesias que nos observan para ver si realmente estamos trayendo a Jesús y el amor de Jesús al mundo. Cuando abrimos nuestros corazones y le damos amor a las personas, estamos entrando en una relación más profunda. Como hijos e hijas de Dios, como seguidores de Jesús, como creyentes, tenemos vida, tenemos amor, tenemos esperanza, tenemos un futuro.

El amor es lo que nos mantiene en marcha. El amor es lo que anhelamos. El amor es lo que la mayoría de nosotros buscamos en una comunidad y especialmente en una iglesia.

Por eso es tan importante el amor. A medida que estamos estableciendo relaciones respetuosas, ofreciendo excelentes opciones en adoración, participación comunitaria y recursos, y mientras estamos siendo legítimos, envolvemos todo en amor. Cuando recordamos que el amor es el camino, y cuando aseguramos a los demás que son amados, el amor de Dios puede cambiar vidas. Todos podemos contar historias de alguien que nos transformó con su amor. Algunos de nosotros hemos tenido líderes de fe que nos han moldeado al mostrarnos amor incondicional. Otros hemos tenido ejemplos de amor en nuestros hogares. Estas experiencias nos han ayudado a querer dar ese amor a otras personas que lo necesitan.

El amor cubre una multitud de pecados, dice la Biblia. Debido a que cubre muchos pecados, cubre muchas otras cosas—incomodidad, confrontación, argumentos, desacuerdos y errores. El amor nos lleva a ser una familia. Lo importante de ser familia es que podemos compartir, estar en desacuerdo, estar de acuerdo, y todos seguimos perteneciendo a la familia, incluso cuando es difícil.

Intenta recordar el momento en que te diste cuenta de que Dios te amaba. ¿Cómo te sentiste? ¿Cómo descubriste que Dios te amaba? ¿Alguien te lo dijo? ¿Lo escuchaste en un sermón? ¿Lo leíste en la Biblia u otro libro? ¿La vida de alguien reflejó el amor de Dios tan claramente que tú lo creíste? ¿Lo escuchaste en una canción? ¿Lo sentiste durante una enfermedad o una tragedia? ¿Lo escuchaste de niño, pero no lo creíste hasta que eras adulto? ¿Te has dado cuenta?

Toda la gente alrededor del mundo son nuestros hermanos. Las personas con las que tenemos problemas también son creadas por Dios y amadas profundamente por Dios. Nuestros hermanos están en otras religiones, tradiciones, países y culturas. Nuestros hermanos y hermanas son homosexuales, lesbianas, transgénero, solteros, gordos, flacos, buenas, malas—hay de todo en nuestra familia mundial. Jesús nos llama, bueno realmente nos ordena, a amarlos. Sin excepciones.

Wendy Pineda estaba buscando un lugar para celebrar su quinceañera un mes antes de cumplir quince años. Esto es muy inusual porque la gente pasa meses, o años, planificando la celebración elaborada y tradicional. Sabía que necesitaba una iglesia para celebrar la misa, una de las partes importantes de la quinceañera. Buscó una iglesia católica romana porque allí iban sus padres una o dos veces al año. Se había bautizado y había celebrado su primera comunión en una iglesia católica romana cerca de su casa, pero no recordaba la última vez que había ido a misa.

Su mamá trabajaba en una escuela y una amiga del trabajo se enteró de que estaba buscando un lugar para tener la quinceañera de Wendy. Le contó de la iglesia a la que asistía, San Mateo, que estaba muy cerca. Le dijo a la mamá de Wendy que estaba segura de que San Mateo haría su quinceañera y que no tenían muchos requisitos. La iglesia a la que Wendy había ido antes requería al menos dos años de asistencia antes de tener una quinceañera.

La primera vez que Wendy fue a San Mateo fue el 31 de octubre; tenían un concierto. Cindy Castellanos tocaba el saxofón y también hizo un rap. Wendy nunca había escuchado o visto música así en la Iglesia. Se sentía aburrida en otras iglesias. No sabía que la Iglesia podría ser divertida. Se sorprendió y siempre recuerda esa experiencia como la primera vez que se encontró con Dios.

Wendy recuerda que, a pesar de que disfrutó su primera experiencia en San Mateo, le iba a dar a la iglesia solo tres semanas—la misma cantidad de tiempo que le tomaría cumplir quince años. Mi papi, el sacerdote, le dijo a la mamá de Wendy que claro que haría su quinceañera y que Wendy tendría que asistir a la iglesia y al grupo de jóvenes durante seis meses—podría hacerse antes y después de la quinceañera. Wendy comenzó a ir al grupo de jóvenes, donde se dio cuenta de que algunos de ellos eran de su escuela. A pesar de que Wendy se sintió bienvenida e incluida, siempre llevaba a su mejor amiga, Lucía Guerrero, con ella como su "manta de seguridad", prometiéndole hacer su tarea de álgebra.

Wendy comenzó a desarrollar una gran relación respetuosa con Alex, mi hermano, que había comenzado el grupo juvenil. Llegaba temprano a la iglesia para conversar con Alex antes de que comenzara el grupo juvenil. Nunca se sintió juzgada por Alex, ni como si tuviera que saberlo todo para ser una líder.

Debido a que su familia no estaba preparada para celebrar la quinceañera, decidieron posponerla y hacer una celebración para sus dieciséis años. Wendy recuerda que sabía que podía dejar la iglesia y regresar seis meses antes de su cumpleaños para prepararse, pero algo cambió durante esas tres semanas que le había dado a San Mateo. Dice que trató de minimizar que le gustaba ir a la iglesia. Le decía a los demás que solo estaba siguiendo las reglas para su inminente celebración y que era por eso que se quedaba.

A lo largo de los años, Wendy comenzó a invitar a amigos cercanos para ir a la iglesia con ella. Ella dice que es difícil lograr que personas sin iglesia vayan a la iglesia, y que por lo general les decía: "Saldré contigo el sábado y haremos lo mío el domingo".

En una ocasión específica recuerda haber llevado a la iglesia a una de sus amigas, Natasha Rodríguez. Como Natasha no acostumbraba a ir a la iglesia, no sabía qué esperar. Todos en la iglesia iban con ropa elegante, pero Natasha fue con pantalones de mezclilla y zapatillas. Natasha se sintió muy incómoda. Para empeorar las cosas, su hijo de tres años comenzó a correr y en un momento corrió hacia el altar. La predicadora levantó al niño y continuó sin parar. Al final del servicio, Anne Grizzle, que había estado predicando, se acercó a Natasha para agradecerle por venir a la iglesia y especialmente por traer a su hijo. Ella empezó a llorar. Wendy dice que este recuerdo es uno de sus favoritos porque Natasha creó relaciones de por vida con otras personas debido a ese primer encuentro muy positivo con la iglesia. "Mirando hacia atrás, puedes ver todos los momentos en que sentiste el amor de Dios y solo te toma un segundo compartir ese amor. Aprovecha cada oportunidad para compartirlo".

Wendy, debido a esos ejemplos, es muy consciente de su lucha por la excelencia en todo lo que hace, especialmente en el ministerio. Ella dice que debemos ser excelentes dentro de nosotros mismos, con nuestros amigos, nuestra congregación y luego con la iglesia en general. "Nunca sabes quién te está observando y nunca sabes cómo la gente se acerca a Dios o la iglesia. Si realmente eres quien dices que eres, la gente a tu alrededor lo notará".

Wendy, a los treinta y cuatro años, todavía está acostumbrada a ser la "joven latina simbólica". Dice que, al principio, era divertido ser la única persona de color y la más joven en los eventos, en el liderazgo o en los equipos de planificación, pero entonces se vuelve triste y decepcionante. Cuando no puede asistir a una actividad, señala: "Siento que tengo que cargar con el peso de proporcionar a las personas los nombres de aquellos a quienes pueden invitar para tomar mi lugar. Eso no es justo, pero espero que las personas que vengan después de mí no tengan que sentir la misma carga".

Su sugerencia es que todos deberíamos rodearnos de personas que son diferentes a nosotros porque si no tenemos un grupo diverso de amigos, estamos perdiendo una gran oportunidad. Si estamos tratando de comunicarnos con otras personas, debemos sumergirnos en esa comunidad y tenemos que hacerlo con todo el corazón porque todos podemos ver cuando alguien está siendo falso o está tratando de usarnos. "Tienes que hablar y escuchar mis necesidades y deseos en lugar de decirme lo que necesito. Eso es importante en todas las relaciones. Tienes que construir una relación para saber cuándo una persona tiene miedo de hablar". Lamentablemente, nos enseñan a ver nuestras diferencias en vez de lo que tenemos en común.

Lo que ha mantenido a Wendy en la Iglesia Episcopal son las profundas y auténticas relaciones construidas con amor. "Ese amor que llena un vacío puede animarte mucho en el momento exacto", dice. El ejemplo de una amistad de amor que tuvo con Alex la ayudó a reflejar eso con sus ahijados. "Esa amistad amorosa y respetuosa con Alex me ha mostrado cómo tratar a una persona más joven. Nunca me sentí estúpida; nunca me sentí como una niña tonta. No puedo precisar ese momento en que nuestra relación cambió para convertirse en amigos de toda la vida, pero eso es lo que quiero con mis ahijados".

El amor ha sostenido a Wendy cuando su mamá se enfermó hace unos años. "Cuando pienso en momentos oscuros, pienso en quién era la luz brillante. En momentos oscuros, diferentes personas me mostraron lo que era el amor de Dios porque necesitaba verlo. Sé que Dios siempre está ahí y siempre me está cuidando, pero necesitaba que me lo recordaran". Y esto incluye el amor de las personas que conoció en San Mateo hace casi dos décadas y que la sostuvieron en momentos muy difíciles, cuando no sabía qué hacer.

Una razón por la que Wendy no abandonará la Iglesia Episcopal, incluso con sus desafíos, es que siente que todavía hay un lugar para ella. No es la misma persona que era cuando llegó a la Iglesia Episcopal a los catorce años. Ha cambiado, ha crecido, sus gustos han cambiado y todavía puede encontrar una comunidad que la acepte y la ame por lo que es en ese momento. "Y en cinco años, cuando haya cambiado un poco más, también encontraré una comunidad; puede que no siempre sea la misma iglesia y la misma comunidad, pero siempre hay un lugar donde encajo".

Wendy ahora es miembro de la junta directiva del campamento Kanuga. Ha estado involucrada en los ministerios de jóvenes, jóvenes adultos, música y latinos/hispanos desde que comenzó a ir a San Mateo. Ha sido parte de los equipos de planificación para los festivales de jóvenes adultos en la Convención General, Nuevo Amanecer y la Reunión de Misioneros Hispanos. También ha impartido talleres y seminarios web sobre la mayordomía y la administración del dinero. Wendy prefiere trabajar desapercibida y aprender la historia tras del trabajo realizado. Profesionalmente, es una exitosa gerente de un equipo de contabilidad en Houston, Texas. Ella continúa usando sus dones, experiencia y conocimiento en la iglesia y más allá. Wendy es un gran ejemplo de lo que producen las relaciones respetuosas, la excelencia, el amor y el ser legítimo.

CHAPTER 6

Now What?

So, now that we have made respectful relationships with people around our neighborhood; we have committed to be excellent in all our communication, liturgies, and events; we have made efforts to be authentic in all we can; and we know that, as followers of Jesus, we have poured unconditional love all around, what is next?

Oh, that is simple; now we grow!

Yeah, it would be great if it were that simple. But it isn't. I have seen growth, both in numbers and in faith. But it is not easy or simple. It is a daily commitment to remain in REAL zone (yeah, this sounds cheesy, but stay with me).

There is a church in Houston that is growing. Their pastors tell me they don't know why they are growing. I think it is simple: they are doing things that other churches in their area may not be. They actually deliver a welcome bag to anyone who fills out their visitor card, that same Sunday or during the following week. They knock on the door and, if someone answers, give the family the welcome bag, ask if they need any prayer, and leave: a simple, heartfelt, short visit. Members of the congregation told me that they have been growing so much they aren't sure if they will be able to continue this ministry to visitors. I hope they do, as I think it is one of the reasons they are growing.

In this example, they are starting a respectful relationship by inviting visitors to fill out the visitor cards—prominently displayed in the pews with instructions on what to do with the completed cards. The relationship continues when the pastor or member of the congregation pays a visit. The welcome bags are excellent—carefully thought through and updated. The church is authentic in not trying to be someone they are not. They are not copying other churches; they are continually looking for ways to make church the place they have always hoped for. And, of course, their love for their ministry and church is evident in their programs, their willingness to try new things, and their faithfulness. When I visited, I asked if they would like to hear what I saw. They were very grateful and listened—even to the not-so-great parts of my observations—showing humility, maturity, and commitment.

I have seen churches doing amazing things—like the welcome visits—and once they have been successful, stop. Then, they notice their numbers are falling again and can't remember what they did before that worked so well. When we are REAL, we keep tabs of what is working, we are constantly evaluating what we are doing. We review to see if there is something we can do better, more efficiently, or if some practices need to go. This takes time, but it is worth it. I have been on so many diets that have been successful, for a time, and then because I have lost some weight, I return to my regularly scheduled eating patterns. I forget that the only reason my life or weight changed was because I added or subtracted some things. If I don't keep up with that, I can't keep losing weight. If we don't keep track of what we are doing and what is working, we cannot know how to be successful or where the success took a turn.

I see the enthusiasm of church planters when they are first starting. They visit around the neighborhood where they are praying the church will be planted. They knock on doors, they develop relationships with local businesses, they make calling cards and magnets, put "Free Prayer" signs up when they are at the coffee shop, and are constantly making new friends and being an involved neighbor. This enthusiasm and time spent to build up their church is immense and sometimes cannot continue at that level of time or enthusiasm.

It is very difficult to keep doing something that takes so much energy and resources, which is why we need to build community. When a church planter is starting, she may only have her family as the church members, but it is a community. Sooner or later, more people will become "regulars" and they will be able to take the lead.

These basic steps by church planters can be emulated by people who are in established churches. Taking the time to be REAL at the beginning is a great gift. It may be tougher and scarier to start when you've been around for a while. If your church is "dying," it is the right time to start REAL. If your church is "thriving," it is the right time to start REAL. If your church is filled with diversity, it is the right time to start REAL. People are in need of love, forgiveness, reconciliation, empowerment, and peace. We, as people of God and followers of Jesus, are called to be instruments of all of these and more.

Follow-up is most important in church work. While you are using REAL as a rubric for ministry, it may be tempting to go through each value and end with love and think, "Ta-da, we are done!" It is more helpful long-term to have ongoing conversations or evaluations with your vestry or ministry group. Part of the follow-up is to have measurable goals for each value. Keeping records of what you are doing, what is working, and what is not working for each value is very important. Also, keep records of what goals you are reaching and which need more time.

Using REAL, see if you are needing to tweak something in each of the values. For example:

- Respectful relationships
  - Are we inviting people from our community to events in our church?
  - Are we being seen around the community?

- Are we involved in community engagement opportunities?
- Are we meeting neighbors where they are and participating in their activities?

- Excellence

  - Have we made changes in ministries and have those changes been successful?
  - Have we incorporated other hymnals, genres, or instrumentation into our music repertoire recently?
  - Have we evaluated our programs for each age group for areas of improvement?
  - Have we updated our social media presence and websites?

- Authenticity

  - Have we incorporated all the cultures surrounding our neighborhood into our church?
  - Does who we are as a church direct our planning?
  - Do we have a wide range of representative voices at the decision-making table?
  - Does our social media presence show our diversity?

- Love

  - Are we showing Jesus's unconditional love in all we do?
  - Are we taking the time to be God's light to the people in our pews?
  - Are we using our resources to show love to our community?
  - Are we taking care of ourselves and the church volunteers?

Back to the question: What do we do now? We continue to be REAL. We continue establishing respectful relationships with people who don't look like us but look like our community. We continue to strive for excellence even when it seems like everything is against us. We work toward authenticity by including as many people as necessary in our planning. We continue to love like Jesus. Love above all. Love during all. Love after all.

Capítulo 6: ¿Y ahora qué?

Entonces, ahora que hemos formado relaciones respetuosas con las personas de nuestro vecindario; nos hemos comprometido a ser excelentes en todas nuestras comunicaciones, liturgias y eventos; hemos hecho esfuerzos para ser auténticos en todo lo que podemos; y sabemos que, como seguidores de Jesús, hemos dado amor incondicional, ¿qué sigue?

Oh, eso es simple; ahora ¡crecemos!

Sí, sería genial si fuera así de simple. Pero no lo es. He visto crecimiento, tanto en números como en fe. Pero no es fácil ni simple. Es un compromiso diario permanecer en la zona REAL (sí, esto suena cursi, pero dame chance).

Las personas necesitamos amor, perdón, reconciliación, empoderamiento y paz. Nosotros, como pueblo de Dios y seguidores de Jesús, estamos llamados a ser instrumentos de todo esto y más.

El seguimiento es más importante en el trabajo de la Iglesia. Mientras usas REAL como rúbrica para el ministerio, puedes pensar al analizar cada valor: ¡"ya hemos terminado"! Es más útil a largo plazo tener conversaciones o evaluaciones continuas con su equipo, comité, junta y grupo ministerial. Parte del seguimiento es tener objetivos medibles para cada valor. Mantener registros de lo que están haciendo, lo que funciona y lo que no funciona para cada valor es muy importante. Además, mantenga un registro de los objetivos que están alcanzando y cuáles necesitan más tiempo.

De vuelta a la pregunta: ¿Qué hacemos ahora? Seguimos siendo REALes. Continuamos estableciendo relaciones respetuosas con personas que no se parecen a nosotros pero se parecen a nuestra comunidad. Continuamos luchando por la excelencia, incluso cuando parece que todo está en nuestra contra. Trabajamos hacia la autenticidad y el ser legítimos al incluir a tantas personas como sea necesario en nuestra planificación. Seguimos amando como Jesús. Amor sobre todo. Amor durante todo. Amor después de todo.

Small Group Devotional Resources

s you work through this book with a small group, you may wish to begin or end your time together with moments of worship and reflection.

Chapter 1: Why REAL?

Prayer

Heavenly God, we look up to you in this time of change. Allow us to have the courage to do what you are calling us to do at this time. We know you prepare the way and you will see us through. Bless us with an open heart, willing spirit, love, strength, wisdom, courage, forgiveness, and an enthusiasm to learn. We pray this in your loving name. Amen.

Song

Sing the following song or another related to starting something new.

"We Give You Thanks" / "Te agradezco"

We give You thanks

Sandra Montes

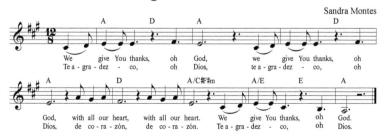

The readings

Read one or more of these passages.

> I hereby command you: Be strong and courageous; do not be frightened or dismayed, for the LORD your God is with you wherever you go.
>
> *—Joshua 1:9*

> It is the LORD who goes before you. He will be with you; he will not fail you or forsake you. Do not fear or be dismayed.
>
> *—Deuteronomy 31:8*

> I am about to do a new thing; now it springs forth, do you not perceive it? I will make a way in the wilderness and rivers in the desert.
>
> *—Isaiah 43:19*

Meditation

Take a moment to share, in pairs or as a group, thoughts on one or more of the above passages.

Reflection questions

In pairs or as a group, answer the following questions.

- Is our church "dying"? Explain.
- Do we need change? Why or why not?
- What are some ways people handle change and transition?
- How can we share our love of God, ourselves, and our neighbors with others?
- Who is the "other" around us? Around our church? Around our neighborhood?

Activity

Take a few minutes to write down what your hopes are for this time of change, transition, evolution. Circle a few words to focus on as you embark on REAL. Take those words with you and meditate on them daily.

The Lord's Prayer

Recite the Lord's Prayer or another appropriate prayer in the language of your heart.

Chapter 2: Respectful Relationships

Prayer

God, we praise you for your great glory manifested in all creation. We praise you for giving us a heart that longs to be in relationship with others. Give us an open heart to embrace all who surround us. Help us to grow in love beyond prejudice, fear, and injustice. Grant us the grace to respect the uniqueness of each person, so that in our diversity we can practice unity. We pray in your Holy Name. Amen.

Song

Sing the following song or another related to respectful relationships.
"I Can Do All Things" / "Todo lo puedo hacer"

Todo lo puedo hacer/I can do all things

Continued

Continued

The readings

Read one or more of these passages.

And let us consider how to provoke one another to love and good deeds, not neglecting to meet together . . . but encouraging one another . . .

—Hebrews 10:24–25

In everything do to others as you would have them do to you; for this is the law and the prophets.

—Matthew 7:12

Honor everyone. Love the family of believers. Fear God . . .

—1 Peter 2:17

Meditation

Take a moment to share, in pairs or as a group, thoughts on one or more of the above passages.

Reflection questions

In pairs or as a group, answer the following questions.

- Do we know our congregation?
- Do we know our neighborhood?
- Have we asked our congregation what they need and want?
- Have we asked our neighbors what they need and want?
- Who are we trying to reach? Why?
- Is our pastor ministering outside of the church at least once a week?
- Is our church welcoming?

Activity

Visit someone and learn something about them. Ask probing questions that will help you get to know them better. Pray for them the rest of the week.

The Lord's Prayer

Recite the Lord's Prayer or another appropriate prayer in the language of your heart.

Chapter 3: Excellence

Prayer

God of all creation, thank you for forming us in your image. Thank you for giving us thoughts, goals, and desires. Help us remember that everything we do is for your glory. Help us strive to honor you in all we do. Thank you for the gifts you have bestowed upon each one of us. Help us be faithful stewards of those gifts. In your name we pray. Amen.

Song

Sing the following song or another related to excellence.

"Do Not Fear" / "No tengas miedo"

No Tengas Miedo

Sandra Montes

The readings

Read one or more of these passages.

> Whatever your task, put yourselves into it, as done for the Lord . . .
>
> —*Colossians 3:23*

Finally, beloved, whatever is true, whatever is honorable, whatever is just, whatever is pure, whatever is pleasing, whatever is commendable, if there is any excellence and if there is anything worthy of praise, think about these things.

—*Philippians 4:8*

Show yourself in all respects a model of good works, and in your teaching show integrity, gravity, and sound speech that cannot be censured . . .

—Titus 2:7–8

Meditation

Take a moment to share, in pairs or as a group, thoughts on one or more of the above passages.

Reflection questions

In pairs or as a group, answer the following questions.

- Are we doing things the same way as when we started this ministry?
- Is the church welcoming (clean, social media/website updated, parking spots for visitors, and so on)?
- Do we think that excellence means perfection?
- Are we planning the music, liturgies, events, and meetings in advance for upcoming liturgical seasons?
- Are we asking people who come visit our church to have an honest conversation of what went right/wrong?

Activity

Think of three people you feel do excellent work or live in excellence. Contact them and try to meet with them in the next week or two. Ask them about their rule of life. If it is a person you do not know, ask or read about them.

The Lord's Prayer

Recite the Lord's Prayer or another appropriate prayer in the language of your heart.

Chapter 4: Authenticity

Prayer

God, Holy Spirit, we pray for a heart filled with humility as we seek to understand the vastness of your creation. We pray for a heart filled with honesty, patience, and discernment to look inside our souls and see our true selves. Help us to accept and love ourselves so we can love and celebrate all who surround us. Please hold us accountable as we seek to live in authenticity and truth. We pray all this in the name of Jesus. Amen.

Song

Sing the following song or another related to authenticity.

"We Are Strong" / "Somos fuerza"

We Are Strong

Sandra Montes

Continued

Continued

The readings

Read one or more of these passages.

> I am reminded of your sincere faith, a faith that lived first in your grandmother Lois and your mother Eunice and now, I am sure, lives in you.
>
> —*2 Timothy 1:5*

> A good tree cannot bear bad fruit, nor can a bad tree bear good fruit. Every tree that does not bear good fruit is cut down and thrown into the fire. Thus you will know them by their fruits.
>
> —*Matthew 7:18–20*

> Therefore be imitators of God, as beloved children, and live in love, as Christ loved us and gave himself up for us, a fragrant offering and sacrifice to God.
>
> —*Ephesians 5:1–2*

Meditation

Take a moment to share, in pairs or as a group, thoughts on one or more of the above passages.

Reflection questions

In pairs or as a group, answer the following questions.

- Are we appropriating multicultural events like *Cinco de mayo* or *Día de Muertos*?
- Are we translating instead of transcreating?
- Is there a reason for including other languages or cultures in our services?
- What voices are we lifting up?
- What leadership are we lifting up?
- Who is around our neighborhood? Are we including them in our worship (liturgy, music, prayers)?
- Are we trying to be someone we are not?

Activity

What three words would the community or neighborhood use to describe your church? Are those three words the same you would use? Why or why not? Are those words being used in your church's mission or vision statements? Share with your leadership team.

The Lord's Prayer

Recite the Lord's Prayer or another appropriate prayer in the language of your heart.

Chapter 5: Love

Prayer

Loving God,

Turn my heart to my neighbor. May my love for my neighbor be as your love—constant, always merciful, patient, welcoming. Help me to love my neighbor as your beloved Son, our brother, does, eternally. May I live in solidarity with them, and with you, forever. Amen.

Song

Sing the following song or another related to love.

"Remain in Me" / "Permanece en Mí"

Remain in Me/ Permanece en Mí

Sandra Montes

The readings

Read one or more of these passages.

> For this is the message you have heard from the beginning, that we should love one another.
>> —*1 John 3:11*

> I give you a new commandment, that you love one another. Just as I have loved you, you also should love one another.
>> —*John 13:34*

> Owe no one anything, except to love one another; for the one who loves another has fulfilled the law.
>> —*Romans 13:8*

Meditation

Take a moment to share, in pairs or as a group, thoughts on one or more of the above passages.

Reflection questions

In pairs or as a group, answer the following questions.

- As Christians, are we following Jesus's command to love God, ourselves, and others?
- Are we committed in our ministries?
- Are we going out into the world because we love our neighborhood or out of obligation?
- Are we feeling comfortable or challenged when we go to church? Why?
- Are we putting others' needs before our own need of doing things the way we've always done them?

Activity

Take God's love to someone who needs it. It could be writing a letter, sending some cookies, or calling a person who is homebound, a busy parent, or a person in your neighborhood who has never come to your church.

The Lord's Prayer

Recite the Lord's Prayer or another appropriate prayer in the language of your heart.

Chapter 6: Now What?

Prayer

All-knowing God, you promise to be with us always, that you will complete the work you began, and that you will provide for all our needs. We turn to you in admiration and hope as we continue to do your will. Please give us vision and passion for this work. In your beloved name we pray. Amen.

Song

Sing the following song or another related to unity and community.

"We Are One" / "Somos uno"

We Are One/Somos Uno

Sandra T. Montes

The readings

Read one or more of these passages.

> Trust in the LORD with all your heart, and do not rely on your own insight. In all your ways acknowledge him, and he will make straight your paths.
>
> —*Proverbs 3:5–6*

> So, whether you eat or drink, or whatever you do, do everything for the glory of God.
>
> —*1 Corinthians 10:31*

> So let us not grow weary in doing what is right, for we will reap at harvest time, if we do not give up.
>
> —*Galatians 6:9*

Meditation

Take a moment to share, in pairs or as a group, thoughts on one or more of the above passages.

Reflection questions

In pairs or as a group, answer the following questions.

- What is our hope for the future?
- What has surprised us during our time reading about/becoming REAL?
- What have we learned as a church?
- Working on becoming REAL may be very difficult; how have we stayed focused on Jesus and his command to share our stories with others and love?
- What has been life-giving? What has been frustrating?

Activity

As you reflect on your REAL work thus far, meditate on your time devoted to REAL. Look back at the list of words you circled during the "Why REAL?" activity and ponder why you wrote those down. During the next week, write a reflection of what you have learned, what you will do or have done, what has worked, what didn't quite work as you hoped, and other insights. Give it to God. And share with others.

The Lord's Prayer

Recite the Lord's Prayer or another appropriate prayer in the language of your heart.

CPSIA information can be obtained
at www.ICGtesting.com
Printed in the USA
BVHW050007020522
635848BV00024BA/386

9 781640 652484